AQA Religiou Studies A

Islam: Ethics

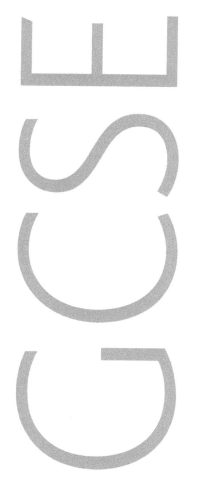

ISSY R

Kim Hands

Peter Smith

Series editor

Cynthia Bartlett

OXFORD
UNIVERSITY PRESS

OXFORD
UNIVERSITY PRESS

Great Clarendon Street, Oxford, OX2 6DP, United Kingdom

Oxford University Press is a department of the University of Oxford.
It furthers the University's objective of excellence in research, scholarship,
and education by publishing worldwide. Oxford is a registered trade mark of
Oxford University Press in the UK and in certain other countries

British Library Cataloguing in Publication Data
Data available

978-1-4085-0477-2

10 9 8 7 6 5 4 3

Printed in Great Britain by Ashford Colour Press Ltd, Gosport, Hants

Acknowledgements

Cover photograph: Corbis
Illustrations: Rupert Besley, Paul McCaffrey (c/o Silvie Poggio Artists Agency),
Pantek Arts Ltd and Dave Russell Illustration
Page make-up: Pantek Arts Ltd, Maidstone

The authors and publishers wish to thank the following for permission to use copyright material:

Alamy: 3.5B, 3.4D, 3.6B, 5.1A, 5.10A, 6.3C, **Corbis:** 2.5 B, 3.2A; **Fotolia:** 1.1A, 1.2B, 1.8B, 1.10B, 1.12A,
CO2, 2.1A, 2.9A, 2.9B, 2.10A, 2.10B, 2.11A, CO3, 3.1B, 3.2B, 3.5A, 3.8A, 4.2D, 4.4D, 4.5C, 4.8B, 4.9A, 4.9B,
4.9C, 4.9D, 4.10B, 4.10C, 4.11A, 5.2A, 5.3C, 5.6A, 5.7A, 5.9A, 6.3B, 6.8A, 6.8B, 6.9A, 6.9B, 6.10C; **Getty:**
2.5A, 3.4A, 3.7A, 3.9B, 4.8A; **IFEES:** 4.7A; **Islamic Relief:** 2.6A; **iStockphoto:** CO1, 1.1B, 1.2A, 1.3A,
1.3B, 1.4A, 1.5A, 1.6A, 1.6Bi, 1.6Bii, 1.7A, 1.8A, 1.8C, 1.9A, 1.9B, 1.11A, 1.11B, 2.1B, 2.2B, 2.3B, 2.3C, 2.8A,
2.8B, 3.1A, 3.7B, 3.9A, 3.10A, 3.11A, CO4, 4.1A, 4.1B, 4.1D, 4.2A, 4.2C, 4.3A, 4.3B, 4.4Ai, 4.4Aii, 4.4Aiii,
4.4Aiv, 4.4Av, 4.4Avi, 4.4Avii, 4.4Aviii, 4.4Aix, 4.4Ax, 4.4C, 4.5A, 4.5B, 4.5D, 4.6A, 4.7B, 4.7C, 4.10D, CO5,
5.1B, 5.2B, 5.2C, 5.2D, 5.3B, 5.5A, 5.5B, 5.8A, CO6, 6.1B, 6.2A, 6.2C, 6.3A, 6.4A, 6.4b, 6.5A, 6.5B, 6.6A,
6.7A, 6.10A, 6.11A; **Muslim Aid:** 2.7A; **PA Photos:** 3.6C, 5.7B, 6.1A; **Reuters:** 1.5B; **Rex Features:** 3.6A,
5.6B, 5.4B.

Throughout: Extracts from 'The Holy Quran Translation and Commentary' by Abdullah Yusuf Ali.
Reprinted with permission of IPCI – Islamic Vision, 434 Coventry Road, Small Heath, Birmingham
B10 0UG, UK; 1.2 Extract from *We want to offer Sharia law to Britain*, Clare Dwyer Hogg and Jonathan
Wynne-Jones, Telegraph Online 19 Dec 2008. © Telegraph Media Group Limited 2009; 1.4 Extract from
Al-Nawawi's Forty Hadith trans. David Burrell and Nazih Daher reproduced by permission of the Islamic
Texts Society. © Islamic Texts Society 1997; 2.4 Adapted from Table A.19 in *World Population Prospects:
The 2006 Revision, Highlights* © United Nations (Working Paper No. ESA/P/WP.202. 2007) Reprinted with
permission; 2.8 Quotation from UK Islamic Mission website: http://www.ukim.org/DesktopDefault.aspx

Although we have made every effort to trace and contact all
copyright holders before publication this has not been possible in all
cases. If notified, the publisher will rectify any errors or omissions at
the earliest opportunity.

Links to third party websites are provided by Oxford in good faith
and for information only. Oxford disclaims any responsibility for
the materials contained in any third party website referenced in
this work.

Contents

The publisher has worked hard to make sure that this book offers you the best possible support for your GCSE course.

■ How to use this book

This book covers everything you may need for your course.

Learning Objectives

At the beginning of each section or topic you'll find a list of Learning Objectives based on the requirements of the specification, so you can make sure you are covering everything you need to know for the exam.

> **Objectives**
>
> **Objectives**
>
> **Objectives**
>
> **Objectives**
>
> First objective.
>
> Second objective.

Study Tips

Don't forget to look at the Study Tips throughout the book to help you with your study and prepare for your exam.

> **Study tip**
>
> Don't forget to look at the Study Tips throughout the book to help you with your study and prepare for your exam.

Practice Questions

These offer opportunities to practise doing questions in the style that you can expect in your exam so that you can be fully prepared on the day.

AQA examination questions are reproduced by permission of the Assessment and Qualifications Alliance.

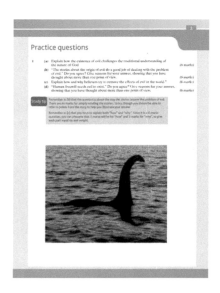

AQA GCSE Islam: Ethics

This book is written specifically for GCSE students studying the AQA Religious Studies Specification A, *Unit 9 Islam: Ethics*. You will be studying six very different ethical topics and the Muslim beliefs and teachings that relate to each of these topics. Many of these teachings are from the *Qur'an* as it is the main written authority in Islam. You do not have to be a Muslim to be successful but an interest in Religious Studies and a willingness to find out more will help you.

Following this unit alone will earn you a GCSE short course qualification in Religious Studies. If you combine it with another unit, you will be eligible for a full course GCSE in Religious Studies. In order to qualify for a grade you will have to sit one 90-minute examination for each unit you study, i.e. for short course, one examination and for full course, two examinations. This is the only form of final assessment.

■ Topics in this unit

In the examination, you will be asked to answer questions based on the following six topics.

Life and death

Issues you will study will include fertility issues, contraception, surrogacy, genetic engineering, abortion and euthanasia. The main Muslim teaching relates to the core idea that life is sacred and special.

Wealth and poverty

Muslim teachings give Muslims a duty to care for the poor. In this topic, you will consider how this is achieved both in poor countries throughout the world and also in Britain. Attitudes to the use of money will also be studied.

Conflict and suffering

This topic includes an understanding of the Muslim beliefs on the purpose of life, justice, reconciliation and peace and how these relate to the concepts of jihad, war and protest.

The environment

This includes such issues as pollution, conservation, recycling and animal rights and how beliefs about stewardship and the value of the natural world influence Muslims.

Crime and punishment

You will be studying what causes crime, what punishment aims to achieve, attitudes towards the death penalty and how Muslim ideas of law, punishment, justice and forgiveness relate to these issues.

Relationships and lifestyle

In this topic you will consider how Muslim beliefs about law, commitment and responsibility influence attitudes to the family, sexuality, social and illegal drugs, gambling, lending money and the role of Islamic schools.

■ Assessment guidance

Your examination will be in two parts. Part A will have four questions split into shorter parts. You will be expected to answer all of the questions in Part A which will total 48 marks.

Part B will contain two further questions. Again, they will be split into smaller parts. You are required to answer one of these, so you will have to choose which one. Each whole question carries 24 marks and it is likely that you will need to give more detailed answers.

Every chapter in this book finishes with assessment guidance, using practice questions. There is also a summary of what you have learnt in the chapter, together with a sample answer for you to mark yourself. Use the large grid opposite to help you to do this.

Examination questions will test two assessment objectives

AO1	Describe, explain and analyse, using knowledge and understanding.	50%
AO2	Use evidence and reasoned argument to express and evaluate personal responses, informed insights and differing viewpoints.	50%

The examiner will also take into account the quality of your written communication – how clearly you express yourself and how well you communicate your meaning. The grid below also gives you some guidance on the sort of quality examiners expect to see at different levels.

Levels of response mark scheme

Levels	Criteria for AO1	Criteria for AO2	Quality of written communication	Marks
0	Nothing relevant or worthy of credit	An unsupported opinion or no relevant evaluation	The candidate's presentation, spelling, punctuation and grammar seriously obstruct understanding	0 marks
Level 1	Something relevant or worthy of credit	An opinion supported by simple reason	The candidate presents some relevant information in a simple form. The text produced is usually legible. Spelling, punctuation and grammar allow meaning to be derived, although errors are sometimes obstructive	1 mark
Level 2	Elementary knowledge and understanding, e.g. two simple points	An opinion supported by one developed reason or two simple reasons		2 marks
Level 3	Sound knowledge and understanding	An opinion supported by one well developed reason or several simple reasons. **N.B. Candidates who make no religious comment should not achieve more than Level 3**	The candidate presents relevant information in a way which assists with the communication of meaning. The text produced is legible. Spelling, punctuation and grammar are sufficiently accurate not to obscure meaning	3 marks
Level 4	A clear knowledge and understanding with some development	An opinion supported by two developed reasons with reference to religion		4 marks
Level 5	A detailed answer with some analysis, as appropriate	Evidence of reasoned consideration of two different points of view, showing informed insights and knowledge and understanding of religion	The candidate presents relevant information coherently, employing structure and style to render meaning clear. The text produced is legible. Spelling, punctuation and grammar are sufficiently accurate to render meaning clear	5 marks
Level 6	A full and coherent answer showing good analysis, as appropriate	A well-argued response, with evidence of reasoned consideration of two different points of view showing informed insights and ability to apply knowledge and understanding of religion effectively		6 marks

Please note that mark schemes change over time. Please refer to the AQA website for the very latest information.

Note: In evaluation answers to questions worth only 3 marks, the first three levels apply. Questions which are marked out of 3 marks do not ask for two views, but reasons for your own opinion.

Successful study of this unit will result in a Short Course GCSE award. Study of one further unit will provide a Full Course GCSE award. Other units in Specification A which may be taken to achieve a Full Course GCSE award are:

Unit 1 Christianity
Unit 2 Christianity: Ethics
Unit 3 Roman Catholicism
Unit 4 Roman Catholicism: Ethics
Unit 5 St Mark's Gospel
Unit 6 St Luke's Gospel
Unit 7 Philosophy of Religion
Unit 8 Islam
Unit 10 Judaism
Unit 11 Judaism: Ethics
Unit 12 Buddhism
Unit 13 Hinduism
Unit 14 Sikhism

1.1 Faith and ethics

Ethics

Ethics is defined as a study of morality which helps to inform people when making decisions about what is the correct action in any given situation. This decision could involve something quite trivial such as whether to eat a bar of chocolate on the way home from school even though you know that it may not be the most healthy option. It could equally be something more important and long-term such as a Muslim refusing to drink alcohol. For a Muslim, making either of these decisions is a matter involving Allah (God) because Allah requires Muslims to look after their body and mind. Eating chocolate is acceptable in moderation, drinking alcohol is not.

Faith and ethics

Islam is a way of life centred on Allah. The main goal of life is to earn a place in Paradise after death, thus maintaining an eternal relationship with Allah which was started at birth. This is achieved through living an ethical life by:

- religious observance, such as obeying the Five Pillars (shahadah – profession of faith; salah – prayer; zakah – alms giving; sawm – fasting; hajj – pilgrimage)
- righteous living, living in such a way that pleases Allah.

This ethical way of life is guided by the teachings in the *Qur'an* and the *Hadith* which Muslims believe are Allah's gifts to mankind. As the *Qur'an* is considered sacred, the way of life it promotes is not widely open to interpretation. As a result many believe the Islamic way of life to be timeless – it can be followed throughout the centuries.

A *Family life and religious observance are important to Muslims*

Key terms

Ethics: the theory relating to what is right and what is wrong behaviour.

Islam: 1) the name of the religion followed by Muslims; 2) to surrender to the will of Allah (God); 3) peace.

Qur'an: the Holy Book revealed to the Prophet Muhammad by the angel Jibril. Allah's final revelation to humankind.

Hadith: the oral tradition relating to the words and deeds of Muhammad.

Sunnah: the words and deeds of the Prophet from the *Hadith*.

Study tip

If referring to the Five Pillars, you can use either the correct English Arabic words (e.g. sawm) or their English meanings (e.g. fasting).

Activities

1. Explain the meaning of the word ethics.
2. a For Muslims the goal of life is to earn a place in paradise by obeying Muslim ethical law. What is your goal in life?
   b Explain why.
   c How are you going to achieve this?

Many Islamic countries are ruled by Muslims in line with their Islamic faith and the teachings of the *Qur'an* and the *Hadith*. The law and legal system in these countries is Islamic so by obeying their country's laws, Muslims are assured of living their lives in a way Allah would approve of. Offences such as murder and rape carry severe punishments, not only because they are destructive crimes but also because they are against Islamic teaching.

Britain is not like this. The British government is a secular government. It allows some practices which Muslims are not allowed to do (e.g. drinking alcohol, lending money with interest charged and dressing 'immodestly'). Thus whilst British Muslims are not forced to break any law to follow their faith, there are some things considered legal which they have to resist. There are a few Muslim members of Parliament who, when ethical issues are debated and changes in the law proposed, put forward Muslim viewpoints. However, they are in a small minority and usually have to follow instructions from their party when voting. In addition, Muslims in Britain have a 'parliament' of their own called the Muslim Parliament of Great Britain. It debates matters of faith and living and has no power to pass laws. Its aim is to work towards creating a caring, informed and morally upright Muslim community in Britain. However, it has no official links to the British government.

B   *The Qur'an – holy book of Islam*

The *Qur'an* is the main Islamic source of religious and ethical authority, containing what Muslims believe to be the words of Allah given to the prophet Muhammad by the angel Jibril.

The *Hadith* is complementary to the *Qur'an*; in some scholars' eyes it clarifies some parts of the *Qur'an*. It is the oral tradition that relates to the words, example and ethical way of life of Muhammad. This is where information about the Islamic way of life (Sunnah) is obtained. This was passed on through word of mouth by Muhammad's followers. Muslims are keen to follow the Sunnah out of respect to Muhammad, whose example they wish to follow.

links

See Chapter 5 for more on crime and punishment.

Research activity

Find out more about the Muslim Parliament of Great Britain at www.muslimparliament.org.uk

Discussion activity

With a partner, discuss whether you think Muslims in Britain should be allowed to do everything which is legal in Britain, even if their faith does not allow it. Give your reasons and be prepared to share your ideas with the class.

Activities

3   Explain the difference between the *Qur'an*, the *Hadith* and the Sunnah.

4   Why do you think Muslims are keen to follow the example of Muhammad?

5   Explain why some people believe that the Islamic way of life can be seen as a little out of date.

Summary

You should now understand the link between faith and ethics with reference to Islam.

1.2 Shari'ah law

Shari'ah law

The *Qur'an* and Sunnah inform Islamic Shari'ah law. The word Shari'ah means 'the path to a watering hole'. It is a religious law which governs areas such as banking, business, contracts, family and social issues. Although Muslims in Britain are subject to British law and the British legal system, Shari'ah arbitration tribunals are allowed as an alternative way of resolving disputes. These are aimed at resolving commercial, civil and matrimonial disputes to the satisfaction of both sides.

Speaking about the possible use of Shari'ah law in Britain, Dr Muhammad Abdul Bari, Secretary General of the Muslim Council of Britain, said:

> ❝ *Shari'ah encompasses all aspects of Muslim life including personal law... In tolerant, inclusive societies all faith groups enjoy some acceptance of their religious rules in matters of their personal life. I am sure some day our society here will also be more at ease with its Muslim community and see the benefit of allowing such rights to those who prefer this.* ❞
>
> *Telegraph Online 19 Dec 2008*

Objectives

Understand and evaluate the place of Shari'ah law in Islam.

Key terms

Shari'ah: Islamic law based on the *Qur'an* and Sunnah.

Discussion activities

With a partner, discuss the quote by Dr Muhammad Abdul Bari. What do you think he is saying? Do you agree with him?

Case study

Shari'ah divorce ruling

Shafina is a British Muslim who is living apart from her husband and wants a divorce so she can remarry. Under British law, there is no problem with her obtaining a divorce but as a Muslim she had a religious ceremony when she married Imran and she feels she wants to abide by Muslim teachings on the process of divorce.

Imran had not been a good husband. He had stolen from her and she discovered that he lied to her on a regular basis. When she challenged him about this two years ago, he left the home they shared. She has since found another partner whom she wishes to marry. Shafina decided to take her case to a Shari'ah court (council) for a ruling by a Shari'ah judge or arbitrator in order that she could divorce according to Shari'ah law, so she would be able to remarry. She was told that there was no problem with her being allowed to divorce given the circumstances of her failed marriage but she would have to wait three months before it could be allowed. When she challenged this, she was quoted teaching from the *Qur'an* which makes it clear that there should be a three month waiting period just in case she was pregnant, in which case the divorce should not be allowed.

Shafina was also told that she should not have considered remarriage until she was 'properly' divorced. However, three months later, her Shari'ah divorce was permitted and later that summer, she remarried.

Beliefs and teachings

When ye do divorce women, divorce them at their prescribed periods, and count (accurately), their prescribed periods:... your women as have passed the age of monthly courses, for them the prescribed period, if ye have any doubts, is three months.

Qur'an 65:1&4

A *Shafina was allowed to divorce and remarry*

Some Islamic countries such as Saudi Arabia and Nigeria use Shari'ah law as their criminal law. This can include some harsh punishments. Execution is the punishment for such crimes as murder, dealing in illegal drugs and adultery. The surgical removal of a hand is a punishment for thieves who repeat their offence. Whilst such punishments exist, they are not used widely because the crime rate in countries where Shari'ah law exists is low. This is possibly because citizens are keen to live their lives in accordance with their Muslim faith.

B *Serious offenders can be executed under Shari'ah law*

Activities

1   What does naming the law 'the path to a watering hole' tell you about the importance of Shari'ah?

2   What is your opinion on waiting three months for a divorce to be granted to take potential pregnancy into account? Give your reasons.

3   'If British law was based on Shari'ah law, the country would be a better place.' Do you agree? Give reasons for your answer showing that you have thought about more than one point of view.

Extension activity

Shafina could have been legally divorced in order to remarry without needing to involve a Shari'ah court. Explain why she involved a Shari'ah court and write down how you feel about her choice.

Summary

You should now be able to understand and evaluate the place of Islamic law in Muslim life.

1.3 The sanctity of life

How is life special?

Activity

1. Spend two minutes writing a list of the ways human beings are more special than any other species.

There should be no doubt in anybody's mind that human life is more special than that of any other species. We can think logically, have developed sophisticated forms of communication and can use our creativity in such fields as art, music and architecture. Humans can choose to follow a faith based on a God. It is unlikely that any other living creature can do any of these things.

However, that does not mean we can abuse other living things just because we are the superior species. Islam has rules and guidelines in place to ensure that Muslims only use other species if it is necessary to advance human life in a way that is pleasing to Allah. They can, for example, eat meat but have to make sure the animal is cared for when alive and then killed humanely.

A   Muslims build beautiful mosques to show their respect for Allah

Why is human life special?

For a Muslim, the fact that life is special leads on to the concept called the sanctity of life. Muslims believe Allah was responsible for creating the original life forms. He has prompted the development of life over millions of years, leading to the situation we have today. This is why life is special – it was first created by Allah and he still takes responsibility for it. This means that no person has the right to damage or destroy life against Allah's wishes. This is an idea that clearly impacts on many issues related to matters of life and death. Of course, it is not quite that simple because nobody can be certain of Allah's wishes, especially in fields of development not specifically

Objectives

Appreciate ways in which life is special.

Understand the ideas of the sanctity of life and the quality of life.

Apply the idea of the sanctity of life and quality of life to matters of life and death.

Key terms

Sanctity of life: the holiness or sacredness of life.

Quality of life: a measure of fulfilment (how good or bad life is in all its aspects).

Discussion activity

Discuss with a partner or small group whether being a member of the superior species affects how other species are treated.

covered in the *Qur'an* and the *Hadith*. In addition, there is still much debate about when life actually begins. Therefore issues like abortion and genetic engineering are more complicated than they may at first appear. However, the *Qur'an* makes it quite clear that not only is Allah in charge of death but he has also decided when that will be.

It can be argued that if a person's life is taken, it may be the predetermined will of Allah that it should be so. However, the principle of the sanctity of life should make this idea open to considerable doubt. To take life is usually regarded as a sin, an act which moves a human being further away from Allah.

> **Beliefs and teachings**
>
> Nor can a soul die except by Allah's leave, the term being fixed as by writing.
>
> *Qur'an* 3:145

> **Study tip**
>
> You should learn this quotation (*Qur'an* 3:145) and use it when writing about Muslim attitudes to death.

Activities

2 Use the quotation from the *Qur'an* 3:145 to explain why Muslims believe in the sanctity of life.

3 Do you think humans can know the predetermined will of Allah? Explain your answer.

The quality of life

In assessing the value of life, many Muslims may consider whether a particular life will be comfortable and free from extreme pain. Others develop this further by asking whether the person will be able to live with freedom, dignity and the possibility of accessing or experiencing Allah. If this is so, this could be seen as good quality of life. However, if their life is unlikely to reach this quality, then perhaps they should be allowed to die. An example of this is a lifesaving operation. Even if the operation will save a person's life, should it take place if the person is going to suffer extreme pain or severe disability for the rest of their life?

Muslims argue that Allah allows people to suffer as a test of their faith but he will not allow them to suffer more than they can bear.

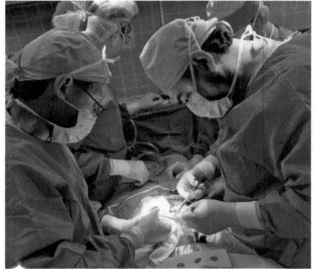

B *Should lifesaving operations take place if they result in a poor quality of life?*

Activities

4 How would you define the 'quality of life'?

5 How does your definition differ (if at all) from how a Muslim may define the quality of life?

Extension activity

Do you think Allah should allow suffering as a test of faith? Give reasons for your opinion.

Summary

You should now be able to appreciate that life is special and understand and apply the ideas of the sanctity of life and quality of life.

1.4 Abortion

Abortion – a definition

The meaning of the word **abortion** is the removal of a foetus from the womb of its mother. This can be natural through miscarriage, with more than 20 per cent of pregnancies ending in this way. However, the word is usually used to refer to the deliberate removal of a foetus under medical supervision. This deliberate removal has aroused much debate for many years, especially from people with religious faith. At one extreme it is seen as the murder of a living being. At the other extreme, it is the removal of what may be seen as a small cluster of cells which, whilst having the potential for life, is not alive when removed. If viewed this way, removal cannot be seen as unlawful killing.

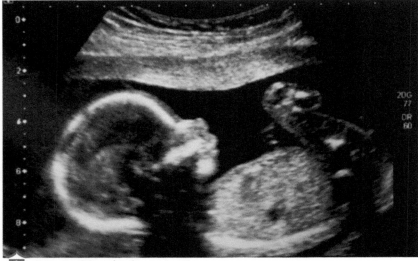

A Foetus at 24 weeks after conception

Between the extremes is a middle way which suggests that abortion is wrong the longer the foetus exists in the womb. British law recognises this by making abortion illegal 24 weeks or more after conception. The exceptions to this are if the baby will be born profoundly physically or mentally disabled or if the mother's life or health is severely threatened if the pregnancy continues. In addition, before 24 weeks, doctors have to be convinced that the potential mother has a good reason, based on certain criteria, for an abortion to be allowed.

Islamic teaching on abortion

Not all Muslims believe the same about abortion. Some believe it is completely forbidden. They follow the teaching in the *Qur'an* to support their belief in the sanctity of life. Humans do not have the right to go against Allah's creative role:

Beliefs and teachings

It is He (Allah) who granteth death and life.

Qur'an 53:44

However, others believe that life does not start at conception so the teaching does not apply. They refer to *Hadith* 4:

Beliefs and teachings

Verily the creation of each one of you is brought together in his mother's belly for forty days in the form of seed, then he is a clot of blood for a like period, then a morsel of flesh for a like period, then there is sent to him the angel who blows the breath of life into him and who is commanded about four matters: to write down his means of livelihood, his life span, his actions, and whether happy or unhappy.

Extract from Al-Nawawi's Forty Hadith trans. David Burrell and Nazih Daher

B

One interpretation of this (which most Muslims follow) is that life begins once the angel has blown the breath of life into the foetus (ensoulment). This comes after 40 days as a seed, a further 40 days as a clot of blood and 40 days as a morsel of flesh, i.e. 120 days or around 17 weeks. Therefore they believe that abortion can take place up to the point of ensoulment provided there is a good reason for it (e.g. the mother's poor health, or rape). As the *Qur'an* suggests, lack of money is not a good reason for abortion:

Beliefs and teachings

Kill not your children for fear of want.

Qur'an 17:31

However, some Muslim scholars believe the first three stages all occur within the first 40 days after conception and that ensoulment occurs soon after. This means that abortion after 6 weeks is prohibited. This all but rules out abortion because most women are unaware that they may be pregnant within the first few weeks after conception.

Discussion activity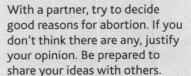

With a partner, try to decide good reasons for abortion. If you don't think there are any, justify your opinion. Be prepared to share your ideas with others.

Activities

1 Explain the different beliefs Muslims hold about when life begins.

2 Which, if any, of these beliefs do you agree with? Give your reasons why. If you disagree with them all, say why.

Case study

Zakra discovered she was pregnant at the age of 32 – 7 years after giving birth to her only child. Although deep down she felt happy, she was concerned because her husband's father lived with them. He had cancer and was becoming more dependent on his son, Zakra's husband. After spending weeks discussing with her husband and her best friend, also a Muslim, Zakra decided to go through with the pregnancy. Her father-in-law died 6 weeks after her baby was born, happy in the knowledge that new life had come to the family.

Summary

You should now know more about abortion and understand how Muslim teachings may influence whether a woman has an abortion.

1.5 Euthanasia

A right to die?

The word **euthanasia** means 'a good death' and is often referred to as 'mercy-killing'. The intention is to help a person who is suffering and perhaps close to death by giving them enough medication to kill them. The main motivation is compassion. This is because euthanasia will prevent them from suffering any further whilst possibly shortening their life only by a few days or weeks.

In Britain, euthanasia is illegal because it could be seen as assisting someone to take their own life (suicide). This is in breach of the Suicide Act 1961. Others believe that people have a right to self-determination and they should have some control over when their own life ends. However, euthanasia involves somebody else at best assisting in the person's death and at worst actually killing them.

A *Euthanasia?*

There are three types of euthanasia. All are illegal in Britain but the first two types of euthanasia are performed in some countries.

- Voluntary – the person asks a doctor to end their life.
- Non-voluntary – the person is too ill to ask but it is believed by a doctor, possibly in consultation with the person's family, to be in the person's best interests.
- Involuntary – disabled, sick and elderly people, for whom life is not seen to have a point, are killed without any consultation just because they are disabled, sick or elderly.

If euthanasia happens, it could be passive or active:

- Passive – this is either where the dose of painkilling drugs, such as morphine, is increased in the knowledge that there is a risk of life being shortened. Alternatively, treatment is withheld or withdrawn because all it is doing is delaying the natural process of dying. Some say that this is not really euthanasia at all.
- Active – giving a drug which will end life, or withholding all treatment with the deliberate intention of ending life.

Activity

1. Working with a partner, think of reasons why some people may be against euthanasia and reasons why others may be in favour of it. Write these reasons down.

Muslim teaching on euthanasia

Muslim teachings on euthanasia are based upon the sanctity of life. Allah gives life and is responsible for it ending. This is all a part of his plan which euthanasia would disrupt. Suffering may be a part of Allah's plan so humans should not interfere with this. If a person expresses a desire to die, they are claiming to know more than Allah by taking the decision from him. In addition, voluntary euthanasia can be seen as suicide, non-voluntary or involuntary euthanasia is classed as murder and all are against the teachings of Allah. Euthanasia could also negatively affect life after death so Muslims are prepared to put up with suffering in order to increase their chances of eternity in Paradise with Allah.

> **Case study**
>
> Adil was diagnosed with motor neurone disease in 2004 when he was 59 years of age. This disease progressively destroys the body's motor neurones – the cells that control voluntary muscular activity, leading to almost total paralysis. It eventually makes breathing impossible. The mind, however, usually remains active and unaffected and this is the condition Adil was experiencing. In June 2008, he heard a feature on the radio about a clinic in Switzerland that offered the opportunity of voluntary euthanasia which allows critically ill people to 'die with dignity'. Under Swiss law, this was perfectly legal.
>
> Adil began to wonder whether this would be an appropriate way to stop him from being what he thought was a burden to his wife and family. When he mentioned it to his wife Samina, she strongly advised him that it was against his Muslim faith and that, despite her love for him, she would not do anything to help him to do this. She also mentioned it to their imam who confirmed that her interpretation of the *Qur'an* was correct. Adil died peacefully at home in November 2008 with his family at his bedside.

B *This machine was used for euthanasia in Australia when it was legal*

⚭ links

For information about the sanctity of life see pages 12–13.

Beliefs and teachings

It is Allah Who gives you life, then gives you death; then He will gather you together for the Day of Judgement about which there is no doubt.

Qur'an 45:26

Activities

2 Explain why many Muslims are against euthanasia.

3 'People should have the right to end their life if their pain gets too much for them.' What do you think? Explain your opinion.

Summary

You should now know about euthanasia and the Muslim attitude to it.

1.6   Fertility issues and contraception

The choice to have children

The opportunity for a couple (and increasingly an individual) to choose whether or not to have children is available to most nowadays. Those who don't want children for any reason can enjoy a full sex life using contraception to prevent the risk of pregnancy. If things go wrong, emergency contraception (the 'morning-after pill') along with abortion are available as an option to consider. However, for Muslims, this doesn't necessarily apply. Children are believed to be a gift from Allah and play an increasingly important role in the family as they get older. There is therefore an expectation that a married couple will have children, although most Muslims are happy for the couple to control when they choose to begin their family.

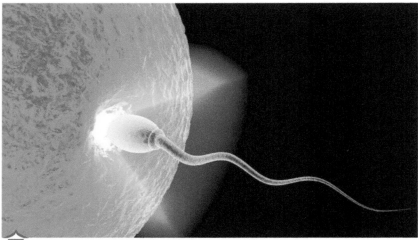

A   A sperm enters a human egg – the beginning of life?

Muslim attitudes to contraception

The *Qur'an* contains no direct teaching about contraception which means Islamic scholars have had to interpret the few teachings that may be relevant. The *Hadith* makes it clear that Muhammad knew of birth control and seemed to approve of it where it was appropriate. In the early 11th century CE, Avicenna, a Muslim physician, listed 20 different substances used for birth control. These were used for several hundred years. However, even then, the most common form of contraception was the withdrawal method. The penis is removed from the vagina before ejaculation takes place, which makes conception unlikely. This is still approved of in Islam although many Muslims insist that the consent of the woman is required. As Islamic ethics forbid sex outside marriage, contraception should be understood in the context of a husband and wife rather than partners, whether long-term or casual.

Objectives

Know and understand the issues of fertility and contraception.

Know and understand Muslim teachings about these two issues.

Key terms

Contraception: the artificial and chemical methods used to prevent pregnancy taking place.

Fertility: the ability to produce children.

Discussion activity

1   With a partner or small group, discuss whether it is right that a married couple should be expected to have children.

Whilst recognising that one of the duties of a married couple is to have a family, most Muslims today support any form of contraception that prevents conception. However, they oppose any form that causes a very early abortion, e.g. the 'morning-after pill'. In addition, they disagree with sterilisation unless there are good medical reasons for it. This is because it permanently prevents a couple having children.

Activities

1 Explain Islamic attitudes to contraception.

2 Explain why you think Muslims oppose contraception that causes a very early abortion, e.g. the 'morning-after pill'.

In the past, people with **fertility** problems were unable to be parents. However, thanks to fertility treatment provided by medical science and technology, this is no longer necessarily so. So have scientists taken over from Allah in deciding who should have children?

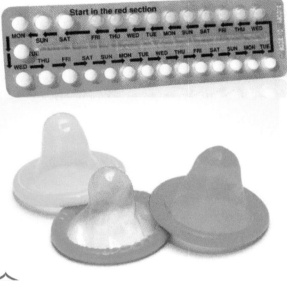

Modern advances in science are causing problems for believers of any religion because the teachings of their founders and in their sacred writings do not refer directly to them. Islam is no exception. Obviously in the 7th century CE when Muhammad lived and when the *Qur'an* was recited to him, modern advances in science were unheard of. Even if Allah had referred to what might happen in the world in the 21st century when speaking to Muhammad (which an all-knowing eternal God would be able to do) nobody would have had the knowledge to understand what he was talking about. Consequently, Islamic scholars have to identify and interpret the teachings they have in the *Qur'an* (e.g. 3:145 on page 13) and the *Hadith* to provide guidance every time scientists announce a new discovery. The field of fertility issues is a good example of this.

B   *Contraceptive pills and condoms*

Discussion activity

2   'Have scientists taken over from Allah in deciding who should have children?' Discuss this question with a partner.

Activity

3   'Nor can a soul die except by Allah's leave, the term being fixed as by writing.' (*Qur'an* 3:145). Make a list of ethical topics for which this teaching can be used for guidance.

Summary

You should now know and understand about fertility issues and contraception, relevant Muslim teaching and Muslim attitudes towards them.

Study tip

It is possible to use the same teachings from the *Qur'an* (e.g. 3:145 on page 13) when writing about different topics, provided that the quotation is relevant to the question.

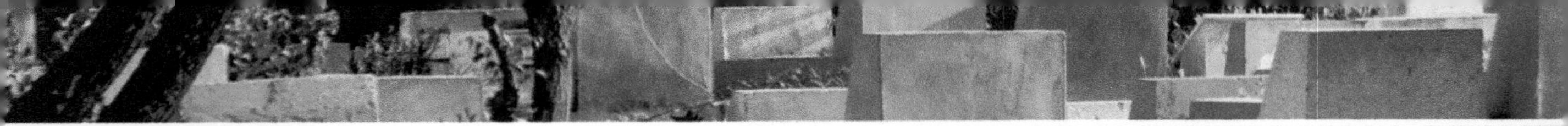

1.7 Artificial insemination

Artificial insemination (AI)

Artificial insemination has been used in farming for many years as an easy way of ensuring animals, especially cows, become pregnant. Without its use, dairy products and meat would be in short supply and more expensive. Similarly, cross pollination of plants helps to increase the supply of crops. Few people seem to mind farmers using these processes but some people express concern about using similar processes with humans.

Human artificial insemination is the process in which sperm is collected from a man and inserted into the uterus of a woman via her vagina. The hope is that fertilisation will take place and she will become pregnant. There are two types of artificial insemination:

- **Artificial insemination by the husband (AIH)** – this is where the sperm used comes from the husband of the woman hoping to become pregnant.
- **Artificial insemination by donor (AID)** (or DI) – sperm is donated (for a small fee) by a male volunteer and, after being screened for diseases such as HIV, is used in the same way as in AIH.

Activities

1. Carefully explain the difference between AID and AIH.
2. Do you think that either of these processes is acceptable? Explain your reasons.

Muslim attitudes to artificial insemination

There are differing views about human artificial insemination.

- Some Muslims believe that Allah bestows children upon married couples as a gift. Not all couples receive this gift. These people should accept their misfortune whilst continuing to live a life of which Allah would approve. Artificial insemination is therefore against the will of Allah. Others believe that Allah is happy for his creative process to be achieved through fertility technology that he inspired people to develop. In the *Qur'an* it says:

Beliefs and teachings

It is He who created you...and made his mate of like nature, in order that he might dwell with her (in love). When they are united, she bears a light burden and carries it about (unnoticed). When she grows heavy (pregnant), they both pray to Allah their Lord, (saying): 'If Thou givest us a goodly child, we vow we shall (ever) be grateful.'

Qur'an 7:189

Objectives

Understand about artificial insemination and Muslim responses to it.

Evaluate Muslim responses to artificial insemination.

Key terms

Artificial insemination: sperm is medically inserted into the vagina to assist pregnancy.

Artificial insemination by the husband (AIH): when a woman is made pregnant by the sperm of her husband, but not through having sexual relations with him.

Artificial insemination by donor (AID): when a woman is made pregnant by the sperm of a man other than her partner, but not through having sexual relations with him.

Study tip

If writing about artificial insemination, it would help to differentiate between the two types.

- Artificial insemination involves masturbation to produce the semen which contains the sperm. Many Muslims forbid this. In the *Qur'an*, it says:

Beliefs and teachings

The believers must (eventually) win through, those... who abstain from sex, except with those joined to them in the marriage bond... but those whose desires exceed those limits are transgressors.

Qur'an 23:1–7

Some Muslims interpret this to mean that masturbation is wrong. However, others point out that it doesn't apply in the case of artificial insemination, especially AIH, because it is within marriage. Masturbation in this instance is not to fulfil sexual desires but to enable the husband and wife to have children as is their duty.

Some very strict Muslims are unhappy with the idea of a stranger being involved in any way in the process of inserting the sperm into the woman's uterus via her vagina. Even though this would be done by a doctor using the sperm from the woman's husband, a strict interpretation could be that it is adultery.

Most Muslims, however, are in favour of AIH being used if it is the only way for a woman to have a child. AID is forbidden though because it breaks the Islamic code of ethics for these reasons:

- The donor is a stranger.
- Inserting the sperm from a man other than the woman's husband could be seen as adultery.
- It allows an unmarried woman to have a child and bring it up on her own.
- It allows homosexual couples to have a child and bring it up in a 'single-sex home'.
- The child may become very upset when they find out their genetic father (donor) is different from the father who brought them up.

Skeikh Muhammad Saleh Al-Munajjid, adds:

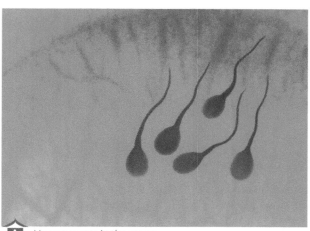

A *Human sperm in the uterus*

> 66 *If a third party, other than the spouses, involves in this process, such as when the sperm comes from another man, then fertilization in such cases is unlawful, because it is counted as Zina or adultery.* 99
>
> www.islamonline.net

Discussion activity

Choose one of the three views on artificial insemination. Spend five minutes discussing it with a partner or small group. Be prepared to share your ideas with other groups.

Activities

3 Which of the five points above do you think a Muslim would consider the strongest argument against AID? Explain why.

4 Do the same for the point that you think a Muslim would consider the weakest.

Summary

You should now know and understand more about artificial insemination and be able to evaluate Muslim attitudes towards it.

1.8   IVF and surrogacy

■ *In vitro* fertilisation (IVF)

Since 1977, *in vitro* fertilisation (IVF) has become commonplace. It has helped couples to become parents who previously would have had no hope of having their own children. The procedure involves the removal of eggs from the body of the mother and fertilising a small number of them, with sperm obtained from the father, outside the body in a glass dish. One or more of the resulting embryos are then medically inserted into the mother. The hope is that one will become embedded into the wall of the uterus and begin to develop and grow, before being born naturally around 38 weeks later. However, success rates are still quite low. Many couples have to undergo treatment several times to achieve success. Some are not successful even after several attempts.

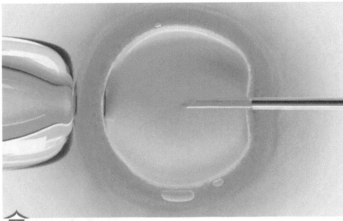

A   *In vitro fertilisation*

Most Muslims are in favour of using IVF if natural conception is not possible. However, it is stressed that only the sperm of the husband and the egg of his wife should be used. There must be no 'third party' involved. That way, the sanctity of marriage is maintained and the resulting child is in no doubt about his or her parentage.

B   *Most Muslims are in favour of using IVF but there must be no third party involved*

Objectives

Know and understand about IVF and surrogacy.

Understand and evaluate Muslim beliefs about IVF and surrogacy.

Key terms

In vitro fertilisation (IVF): a scientific method of making a woman pregnant, which does not involve sex. The sperm and egg are fertilised in a Petri dish.

Surrogate mother: a woman who has a baby for another woman.

Surrogacy: a procedure in which a woman agrees to carry a child conceived artificially for another woman who is unable to do so herself.

∞ links

For more information about Muslim attitudes to IVF, see those related to artificial insemination in pages 20–1.

Discussion activities

1. Discuss with a partner whether IVF should be allowed. Think of **two** reasons why it should and **two** reasons why it shouldn't.

2. After a couple of minutes of discussion, be prepared to share your ideas with the rest of the class. You could then write down the three best reasons for each opinion.

Surrogacy

Fertility treatment can also be used to 'impregnate' a surrogate mother. A surrogate mother will give birth to a child but hand it over to a couple to raise as their own child. It is usual for the surrogate mother's egg and sperm from the intended father to be used via artificial insemination treatment (traditional surrogacy). However, if the intended mother has working ovaries, their 'genetic' child can be conceived through IVF and implanted into the surrogate mother's womb (gestational surrogacy). Once the baby is born, it is handed over to the couple for whom she carried it. Under British law, she can be paid expenses but not a fee.

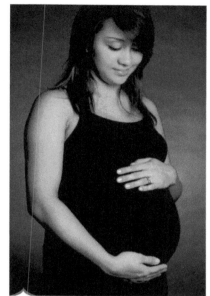

C Some women choose to carry a child for another woman

After the child is born, the intended father will put his name on the birth certificate as the father of the child. This automatically gives him equal rights over the child with the surrogate mother. After six weeks the couple who intend to raise the child can apply for a Parental Order. This give them full parental rights over the child and the surrogate mother loses all the rights she had in the first six weeks.

Muslims are opposed to surrogacy for several reasons:

- Involving a 'second woman in the process' is seen as adultery.
- Family life and identity are very important. If a child's genetic mother is different from the mother who brought them up, the accuracy of the family relationship is affected. This means there is confusion over who the parents actually are. This causes problems regarding inheritance – something that is important to Muslims.
- It is Allah's choice whether a married couple have children and this should not be interfered with. Acceptance of childlessness is a mark of true faith.

Activities

1 Explain the system of surrogacy.

2 Write down why you agree or disagree with each of the three reasons why Muslims oppose surrogacy.

3 'Acceptance of childlessness is a mark of true faith.' Do you agree? Give reasons for your answer, showing that you have thought about more than one point of view.

Summary

You should now know and understand about IVF and surrogacy and understand Muslim attitudes towards each.

1.9 Reproductive cloning

Reproductive cloning

Reproductive cloning is the creation of an identical copy of an organism which could be an animal, a plant or even possibly a human. This technique came to widespread public attention in 1996 when, after hundreds of failed attempts, British scientists cloned 'Dolly' the sheep. Since then a few groups, possibly seeking publicity, claimed to have cloned a human person. Whilst this is possible scientifically, these groups were unwilling or unable to produce the proof of this when challenged.

Research activity

Try to find out more about Dolly the sheep. Would you call the cloning of Dolly a success? Explain the reasons for your answer.

Extension activity

Do you think the cloning of Dolly the sheep was morally justified? Explain your answer.

Reproductive cloning could conceivably provide the 'nightmare scenario' of armies of identical clones, under the command of an evil dictator, taking over the world. Creating a cloned 'master race' would change the human personality and remove the duty to take personal responsibility for one's actions. This would seem to be wrong. Moreover cloned people would lack two parents to provide the genetic family background and identity that is so important to Muslims. Of course the notion of a cloned army would contradict the peaceful ideals of the faith.

Objectives

Know and understand about reproductive and therapeutic cloning.

Understand and evaluate Muslim attitudes to cloning.

Key terms

Cloning: the scientific method by which animals or plants can be created which have exactly the same genetic make-up as the original, because the DNA of the original is used.

Reproductive cloning: to make a complete genetically identical animal, possibly a human being.

Stem cell: a cell, most often taken from a 4–5 day old embryo (blastocyst), whose role in the body is yet to be determined.

Therapeutic cloning: removing cells from a patient and treating them in a laboratory in order to produce stem cells which may be used to treat disorders, e.g. Alzheimer's disease.

A A fictional army of muscular male clones

Fortunately, this scenario is only fictional because there are legal controls in place worldwide to prevent this from happening.

Muslim attitudes to the technology of cloning animals differ. Some Muslims may believe that Allah gives us knowledge and we should therefore use it. However, most Muslims would use Muslim ethical teachings to oppose this sort of reproductive cloning. They would argue that cloning animals interferes with Allah's creative power.

Discussion activity 👤👤👤

'Reproductive cloning is the way forward for the human race because it would control who has a child and eliminate genetic disease.' With a partner, discuss whether you agree with this statement.

Activity

1 Muslims think that humans should take personal responsibility for their actions. Why do you think they consider this to be important?

Therapeutic cloning

Reproductive cloning is not the only type of cloning that is now scientifically possible. There is also the opportunity to use cloning in a therapeutic way – to help to treat a range of diseases. DNA is taken out of an embryo and replaced with DNA taken from another individual in order to generate stem cells. It is sometimes known as stem cell cloning. The aim is to take the stem cells from the modified embryo and use them in research to find treatments for a range of diseases. According to the law, any embryos used in such a way have to be killed after 14 days. Although the theory of therapeutic cloning is sound, scientists will need to do a great deal more work in developing the technique and thoroughly testing the results. This is likely to take many years.

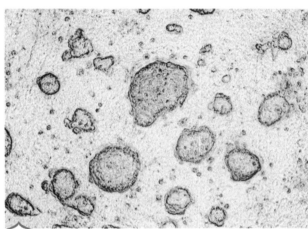

B *Embryonic stem cells*

Whilst many Muslims recognise the benefit of this technology, they are concerned about creating and modifying embryos for such a purpose. This is because they may interpret this as taking the life-giving duty of Allah upon themselves. Consequently, they forbid the creation of embryos specifically for this purpose but will allow extra embryos not used in IVF treatments to be used.

Activities

2 Explain what 'reproductive cloning' and 'therapeutic cloning' mean.
3 Do you think either of these two types of cloning should be used? Give your reasons.
4 If you are not a Muslim, do you think a Muslim would answer Question 3 differently from you? If so, what would be different? If their answer would be the same, why would this be?

Summary

You should now know about two different types of cloning and Muslim attitudes to each.

Study tip

If you are asked to answer a question on cloning, try to include both reproductive and therapeutic cloning in your answer unless the question specifies only one or the other.

1.10 The use of genetic engineering

■ Designer babies

Few people would want to have the option to make choices like the ones in the cartoon. However, it is not impossible that in the future such a choice may be available. American scientists have already produced a genetically modified human embryo. The technology they used could lead to the selection of genes specifying height, intelligence and hair colour, for example. If allowed, this technology could lead to designer babies where parents could choose the gender and characteristics they would like their baby to have.

Most scientists in the field of human genetic engineering insist that the purpose of their work on human embryos is to find ways of curing human diseases caused by faulty genes. It could also enable them to select healthy, disease-free embryos to implant in a potential mother's womb.

We want an intelligent boy with dark hair, brown eyes and a lovely smile. Being good at football would be nice.

A

■ Saviour siblings

Case study

In June 2003, Daniel Cartwright was born in Cambridge. He was conceived by IVF for a very good reason. His brother had a rare and potentially fatal form of anaemia. However, this could be cured by a transplant of stem cells from a saviour sibling with a perfect match. Doctors identified embryos which they believed were disease free and a perfect tissue match. After Daniel's birth, stem cells were collected from his umbilical cord under the supervision of doctors. The intention was to use them to cure Daniel's brother.

This case (and others like it) raises many religious and ethical issues arising out of having a child with the intention of using his stem cells to help cure a sibling.

The Human Fertilisation and Embryology Act of 2008 made the use of saviour siblings legal. Stem cells from the donor sibling must be collected in a way that does not harm them (as in the case study). However, it is illegal to use the donor for organs such as a kidney. (Note: the human body can cope with just one kidney even though it has two.) As with other uses of embryos, the embryos that are not implanted in the mother have to be destroyed no later than 14 days after conception.

Somatic cell therapy

Somatic cell therapy involves introducing new genetic material into cells to correct an absent or faulty gene which causes a genetic illness. This can be done in three ways:

- Ex vivo – cells are removed from the patient, genetically altered and put back into the patient.
- In situ – this requires cells including DNA from elsewhere to be placed directly into affected tissue.
- In vivo – similar to 'in situ' but the cells are placed in the bloodstream. They then find the 'target tissue' so they can deliver the new genetic material to it.

Muslim responses

Many Muslims believe that whilst scientific advances are mainly good, there are limits governed by religious and ethical guidelines. Simply, if scientific advances result in the advancement or improvement of human life, they are welcomed provided the methods used conform to Muslim religious and ethical guidelines. Thus genetic engineering and embryo research are acceptable provided embryos used are not created specifically for research and they are destroyed at an early stage.

> **Beliefs and teachings**
>
> If any one saved a life, it would be as if he saved the life of the whole people.
>
> *Qur'an* 5:32

However, using technology to create designer babies is not acceptable. This is because it doesn't benefit mankind. Also if it is used to select the gender of the resultant baby, this removes the creative choice of Allah. There are some Muslims who believe that our genetic make-up is determined by Allah and any attempt to change this is in opposition to Allah's wishes.

Study tip

If you are asked a question about somatic cell therapy, you do not need to memorise the names of the different types.

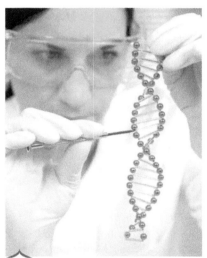

B   *Are genetic scientists just 'playing God'?*

Activities

3 Explain what somatic cell therapy is.

4 What does the quotation from the *Qur'an* 5:32 tell you about what Muslims believe about genetic engineering?

Extension activity

'Any technology that helps people to have better and more enjoyable lives has to be good.'

What do you think about this statement? Give reasons for your answer.

How do you think a Muslim would respond to this statement? Explain why.

Summary

You should now know and understand about three different types of genetic engineering and Muslim attitudes towards them.

Life after death

A   *A Muslim cemetery*

A key consideration when considering matters of life and death concerns what happens after death. This affects each person who faces death because death is inevitable. However, it also affects a person who may feel it is right to take life by euthanasia or deny a foetus the chance of life through abortion. Muslims call life after death akhirah.

Origins of the belief

Muslims believe that humans are sent to earth for a reason and are accountable to Allah for what they do in their life. Adam was the first person on earth. He was promised that if he followed Allah's instructions whilst on earth and became a true servant of Allah, on **Judgement Day** he would be physically resurrected and receive favourable judgement to allow him into heaven. All Muslims believe that the same will apply to them. Heaven (jannah) means eternity with Allah. Hell (jahannam), for some, could possibly be a place of temporary purification of their wrongdoings before they join Allah in heaven. For others, hell may mean eternal punishment.

Beliefs and teachings

On that Day will men proceed in companies sorted out, to be shown the deeds that they (had done). Then shall anyone who has done an atom's weight of good, see it! And anyone who has done an atom's weight of evil, shall see it.

Qur'an 99:6–8

Heaven and hell

There are believed to be different levels in heaven so even after death, Muslims are still on their journey towards Allah. These levels can be moved through, for example, by bringing up a faithful child whilst alive and, once dead, by having living Muslims offering sincere prayers for the dead. Living a life worshipping Allah and following his ethical teachings are essential in order to reach heaven, follow through these levels and achieve an eternal life with Allah.

Resurrection is physical so Muslims bury the dead within 24 hours of death if possible. Cremation is not practised in Islam. When the body is first buried, two angels Munkir and Nakir ask the dead person four questions:

- Who is your God?
- What is your religion?
- Who is your prophet?
- What is your guide?

Answering these questions correctly and truthfully will fill the tomb with pleasurable things. However, if any are incorrect, the dead person will be punished for being a non-believer. Once the trial is complete, the angel of death Azrail takes the souls to Al-Barzakh. This is a place where they will wait for Judgement Day. On Judgement Day, all bodies will be resurrected and will be judged by Allah before being rewarded in heaven, pictured as a paradise garden, or punished in the fires of hell.

B   *Heaven is pictured as a paradise garden*

> ### Beliefs and teachings
>
> In the Garden of Bliss... (They will be) on Thrones encrusted (with gold and precious stones), reclining on them, facing each other. Round about them will (serve) youths of perpetual (freshness), with goblets, (shining) beakers, and cups (filled) out of clear-flowing fountains.
>
> *Qur'an* 56:12, 15–18

The promise of heaven and the threat of hell provide Muslims with a strong motivation to live their lives in a way Allah would approve of. If they break the rules, the punishment may be eternal. The problem comes with the interpretation of the will of Allah, however. Most topics in this chapter are not referred to specifically in the *Qur'an* and the *Hadith*. If Muslims end up doing the wrong thing through thinking that their interpretation is correct when it is actually against the will of Allah, they have to rely on Allah's mercy for their final destiny.

Research activity

Look at the *Qur'an* 56 for more information about Judgement Day.

Activities

4   Explain the link to show how Muslims believe life before death influences life after death.

5   What other motivations are there to live a good life? Are they as strong as the promise of heaven and the threat of hell?

Study tip

It is important that you link ideas about heaven and hell with how Muslims are expected to behave whilst alive.

Summary

You should now know and understand Islamic ideas about life after death and be able to link them to life before death.

1

Life and death – summary

For the examination, you should now be able to:

✔ understand how Muslim principles on the purpose, quality and sanctity of life influence attitudes to:
  – abortion
  – euthanasia
  – contraception
  – fertility treatment
  – surrogacy
  – reproductive cloning
  – stem cell (therapeutic) cloning
  – genetic engineering
  – saviour siblings
  – designer babies
  – somatic cell therapy
  – life after death, resurrection and judgment

✔ apply relevant Muslim teachings to each topic

✔ give your own opinions about each topic and be able to evaluate them from different points of view.

Sample answer

1 Write an answer to the following examination question:
   Describe Muslim beliefs about euthanasia.   (6 marks)

2 Read the following sample answer:

> Muslims disagree with euthanasia. They believe that Allah gives life and only Allah can decide when to take it away. This is called the sanctity of life. If someone is suffering, they have to accept it because it is Allah's decision that they should suffer. Murder is wrong anyway.

3 With a partner, discuss the sample answer. Do you think that there are other things that the student could have included in the answer?

4 What mark would you give this answer out of 6? Look at the mark scheme in the Introduction on page 7 (AO1). What are the reasons for the mark that you have given?

Practice questions

1   Look at the photograph and answer the following questions.

    (a) Why might some Muslims be in favour of in vitro fertilisation (IVF)?   *(4 marks)*

> **Study tip** Try to include at least one piece of specific Islamic teaching to support the reasons you are giving.

    (b) Give **two** reasons why a Muslim may oppose artificial insemination by donor (AID).   *(4 marks)*

> **Study tip** When a question asks you to give two reasons, you will earn 1 mark for each reason (provided they are correct) and 1 mark for explaining or developing it (4 marks in total).

    (c) 'It is Allah, and not people, who is in charge of matters of life and death.' Do you agree? Give reasons for your answer, showing that you have thought about more than one point of view.   *(6 marks)*

> **Study tip** Before you start writing, think carefully of reasons why some people think Allah is in charge of matters of life and death and reasons why some people think people are in charge of matters of life and death.

2.1 Care and the community

Introduction

As you sit in your classroom, you may have a bottle of drinking water on your table or in your bag. Meanwhile, there are millions of people in the world whose daily routine is to go to their nearest stream and bring back enough water for their family to use. They may even have a wash in the stream before they collect the water from it. After all, other people and animals do exactly that. For them, a bottle of clean, pure, chilled water seems like an impossible dream.

A *In many places, people and animals use the same water*

Using water from a stream in these conditions means that people are likely to pick up diseases, such as cholera and dysentery. These are carried in dirty water but as there is no alternative, it is a risk worth taking. Why should billions of people have to take this risk?

In addition, people in parts of the world where there is little water are likely to struggle to grow sufficient food to provide for themselves and their families. Therefore, partly as a result of disease and partly because food is scarce, their life expectancy is much lower than it is in Britain.

Muslim teaching on caring and the community

The basic community unit in Islam is the family. It is the responsibility of more wealthy family members to care for the less wealthy members. However, this cannot work if the whole family is suffering through poverty. Yet the *Hadith* tells Muslims:

He who eats and drinks while his brother goes hungry is not one of us.

Hadith

The interpretation of 'brother' here does not necessarily mean literally a member of the close family; Muslims talk about all fellow-Muslims as brothers. This statement shows that Muslims should take responsibility for helping each other.

The idea of community that this encourages is important. Muslims call their community the **Ummah**. There is some dispute about who is included in the Ummah. Most Western Muslims (and many from the East) interpret it as meaning the whole worldwide Muslim community. However, some use it to refer to collective nations of Islamic states. Whichever interpretation a person takes, it establishes a great feeling of brotherhood and sisterhood in the faith.

This brotherhood or sisterhood gives Muslims all over the world a great feeling of support. If they are struggling with a particular element of their faith, either

B *A market scene*

religious or ethical, they know that it is likely that they will not be alone in their struggle. The annual fast during the month of Ramadan is made easier by the knowledge that there are hundreds of millions of Muslims in the same situation. They are all reminding themselves of what it is like to be hungry.

The concept of the Ummah is reinforced in the *Qur'an*:

Let not the believers take for friends or helpers unbelievers rather than believers: if any do that, in nothing will there be help from Allah: except by way of precaution, that ye may guard yourselves from them.

Qur'an 3:28

This does not prevent Muslims having friends who are not Muslim. However, it advises them that in matters of faith and ethics, help and advice should come from their community of fellow Muslims – the members of the Ummah.

Summary

You should now understand about issues of wealth and poverty and Muslim concepts of caring and the community.

2.2 Characteristics of Less Economically Developed Countries (LEDCs)

What is a Less Economically Developed Country?

A **Less Economically Developed Country (LEDC)** is a country which is termed as poor and in need of help from richer countries like Britain. In the past, they have often been referred to as 'third world' countries but that term tends to be used less nowadays. (A More Economically Developed Country is an MEDC.)

The term LEDC refers to the economic development which is an indication of how rich the country is. If a country has industries or business skills that other countries need and they can trade with these countries, they have a stronger economy than if they do not produce goods to trade. If the country sells more than they buy, their economy will be stronger still. If they have valuable resources that the rest of the world needs (e.g. oil), they can quickly develop their economy and provide a higher standard of living for their people.

However, LEDCs are largely not able to produce sufficient goods to trade and many do not have resources other countries need. As a result the people who live there are poor. Even if they have resources such as oil or minerals, they often do not have the machinery or qualified skilled personnel to extract them. They may also lack pipelines or road and rail systems to transport these resources to centres of population, where they can be used, or to ports for export overseas. As a result the government may sell the rights to the resources to a **More Economically Developed Country (MEDC)** that does have the machinery and personnel. These rights are generally sold for less than the LEDC would earn if they were able to exploit them themselves.

Where in the world are LEDCs?

Objectives

Know and understand the characteristics of a Less Economically Developed Country.

Analyse what life is like in a Less Economically Developed Country.

Key terms

Less Economically Developed Country (LEDC): a country lacking sufficient economic development to lift people out of poverty.

More Economically Developed Country (MEDC): a country where economic development allows people to enjoy a comfortable standard of living.

⚭ links

See pages 36–37 for information about Sudan, an example of an LEDC that has been able to exploit its natural resources.

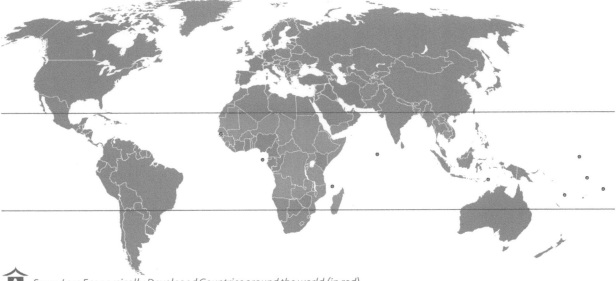

A Some Less Economically Developed Countries around the world (in red)

As map **A** shows, many LEDCs lie between the tropics of Cancer and Capricorn where resources are scarce. Some of this land, especially over large areas of central Africa, is desert. This land does not have easy access to the resources the world needs, nor can the people grow enough crops to eat and find sufficient water to drink. Therefore such desert regions have few people living in them. Most of the population is crowded into the cities which have grown up in areas which are easier to develop.

Muslims form the majority of the population in many African LEDCs, e.g. Somalia, Mauritania, Senegal and Niger. This provides a challenge to the unity of the Ummah. There are many Muslims struggling to find food and water in these countries. Despite giving financial and practical support, the worldwide brotherhood of Muslims, as with the rest of the world, seems unable to cope with the scale of the problem.

B   *Camels in the Tenere desert, Niger*

Summary

You should now know and understand what an LEDC is and be able to analyse what life is like for people living in an LEDC.

2.3   Causes of poverty (1)

Introduction

There are several reasons why some countries in the world are affected by poverty. Some reasons are linked to natural causes, such as earthquakes or drought. Other reasons are influenced by people, sometimes people living in the country themselves and sometimes people living in richer, more economically developed countries.

Location

As map A shows, a country's geographical location can affect its wealth. This may be partly due to its climate but also whether it has natural resources like oil and minerals that richer countries want to buy.

Countries in the Middle East and central Africa have a climate that is very hot and dry. This climate normally leads to poverty because people living there have problems growing enough crops to feed themselves and their farm animals. However, because they have large reserves of oil within their boundaries, some countries are very wealthy. Saudi Arabia has 25 per cent of the world's oil discovered so far.

Saudi Arabia (an MEDC) is separated from Sudan (an LEDC) by a relatively narrow stretch of the Red Sea. However, as pictures B and C show, Saudi Arabia is a rich country due to its oil reserves, whereas historically, Sudan has been very poor. However, over the last few years, the economy of Sudan has been growing quickly. This is because, since 1999, Sudan has been exporting oil. This has encouraged the development of light industry, and trade with the rest of the world has increased greatly. In 2007, Sudan had the world's 17th fastest growing economy. As a result, infrastructure, such as roads and oil pipelines, has been developed and now the country's rich mineral deposits are being mined and traded. However, China, Malaysia and India each have large stakes in the oil industry. The Sudan National Petroleum Company owns just five per cent of the biggest company involved in the Sudanese oil fields. Therefore much of Sudan's oil wealth goes overseas rather than helping its people.

Despite this growth, civil war and a harsh climate including regular droughts have left millions of Sudanese people very poor. They have not been able to get crops to grow in often bare or dry soil. When they have been able to grow the crops, they are dependent on the rain continuing to fall. Economic developments have not affected them greatly. Because the impressive growth figures are based on a very low level of development, and because much of the oil revenue goes to overseas companies, Sudan is still an LEDC.

The average life expectancy in Sudan is 57 years for men and 60 years for women, whilst in Saudi Arabia it is 71 years for men and 75 years for women.

A   *Neighbouring countries Saudi Arabia and Sudan*

B   *Riyadh in Saudi Arabia*   **C**   *A refugee camp in Sudan*

Politics

Although they are both predominantly Islamic countries, Saudi Arabia and Sudan are run in different ways. Saudi Arabia has a relatively stable government. The country is led by a king, currently King Abdullah, who oversees a constitution based on Shari'ah law. There are no recognised political parties or national elections (although men voted in local elections in 2005) and most citizens of Saudi Arabia seem happy with this situation.

Government in Sudan is also based on the authority of one man, the President, but it lacks the stability of Saudi Arabia. For twenty-five years a civil war raged between the Muslim, Arabised North; and the Christian and African South. Two million people died before a peace deal was signed in 2005. Alongside that, the Darfur conflict in western Sudan began in 2003. So far this conflict has cost over 200,000 lives and made two million people refugees. There is evidence that pro-government militias have been carrying out **ethnic cleansing**. This means the systematic killing of one **race** of people by another, for reasons purely based on race or nationality.

Activity

1   Draw a table like the one below. Research information about Saudi Arabia and Sudan from these pages and from the internet. Then add facts about the location, climate, resources, wealth, life expectancy and politics to this table.

	Saudi Arabia	Sudan
Location		
Climate		
Resources		
Wealth		
Life expectancy		
Politics		

Activities

2   Find causes of poverty in these pages. List them and decide whether they are natural or caused by people. You may decide that some are both natural and caused by people. Can you think of any other causes of poverty?

3   Which of these causes do you think results in the greatest poverty? Explain why.

Summary

You should now be able to discuss some of the reasons which may cause a country to be rich or poor and understand that whilst some causes are natural, others are caused by people.

2.4 Causes of poverty (2)

Climate

One of the biggest causes of poverty is climate. In order to grow crops to eat or to feed animals, a certain amount of rainfall is needed. However, in some countries in Central and Eastern Africa, such as Somalia, Chad and Mali, rainfall is very scarce at the time when it is needed. Indeed, 92 per cent of the African continent has insufficient rainfall to assist farmers. Summers are very hot, baking the dry arid land and making it impossible to plant, water and grow crops. More importantly, such drought conditions mean there is insufficient water for people to drink. Because the countries are poor, they often do not have the facilities to collect and keep the water that falls during the rainy season for when it is needed.

Scientists estimate that global warming is making matters worse. The dry regions of the world are becoming drier and the wet regions are becoming wetter. This trend is likely to continue, resulting in millions of people facing the real prospect of starvation. Unless rich countries give them aid, or unless different systems can be introduced, the most affected countries will be unable to cope with such extremes of climate. These systems could include more efficient irrigation systems that ensure water is not wasted or facilities to store water during a rainy season so it can be used all year round. In 2006, over 25 million people in sub-Saharan Africa faced a food crisis and the figure is rising year on year.

However, the real need is for a reversal of global warming, much of which is caused by industrial activity and the demand for cheap energy from non-renewable resources such as gas and oil in MEDCs. This is a large factor in climate change. It is ironic that the countries that are suffering most through climate change are LEDCs; they are hardly contributing to global warming, compared with many MEDCs which are.

Population growth

Another cause of poverty is population growth, especially in countries that can least afford extra mouths to feed. Most rich countries have a stable population with roughly as many babies born as people dying. However, in poor countries, the lack of contraception means that the population is increasing. In addition, with the possibility of babies dying in infancy, people are likely to have more children. This is to ensure they have someone to help the family live from day to day and to care for them in later life. The figures relating to the rate of death in infancy are called the infant mortality rate.

Economic reasons

The system that governs what countries buy and sell to each other, and the price they are able to charge, does nothing to help most inhabitants of poorer countries. Producers of crops like wheat and rice sell their

Objectives

Investigate some further causes of world poverty.

Evaluate causes of poverty.

Key terms

Aid: to help or assist people in need, usually by gifts or money. Most people think of this as donating to charities that provide help to the poor, particularly in the developing world.

Infant mortality rate: the rate at which small children die.

A *Infant mortality rates*

Country	Number of live births per thousand that die by their fifth birthday
Mali	199.7 approx 20%
Somalia	192.8 approx 19%
Chad	189.0 approx 19%
The World	73.7 approx 7%
United Kingdom	6.0 approx 0.6%

Adapted from Table A.19 in World Population Prospects: The 2006 Revision, Highlights, United Nations

Extension activity

Spend two minutes writing down how the figures in Table A make you feel then share your feelings with a partner.

Study tip

You will not be expected to quote figures, but it will help if you show that you know that there are big differences between countries and understand possible reactions for this.

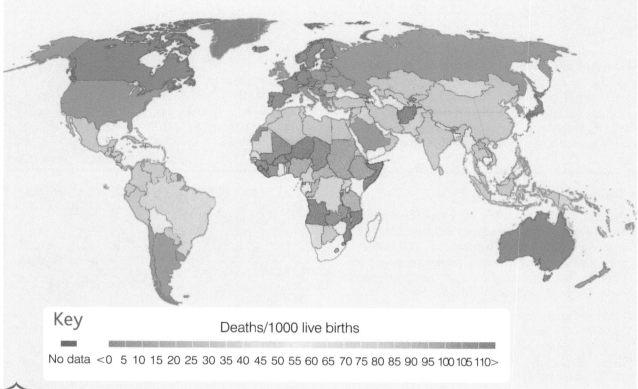

Key   Deaths/1000 live births

No data <0 5 10 15 20 25 30 35 40 45 50 55 60 65 70 75 80 85 90 95 100 105 110>

B   *Infant mortality rates around the world, 2007; the overall rates disguise the fact that there are variations within each country from one region to another, as in Chad, Mali and Somalia*

crops to the country that pays the most for them. This means that poor countries, that cannot afford to compete with rich countries on the open market, cannot buy such crops to feed their people. Consequently, they have to depend on what they can produce themselves. The self-production in these countries is hindered by wealthy farmers using valuable agricultural land to grow cash crops such as fruit, flowers and vegetables that they can sell to rich countries. The profit they earn doesn't benefit the poor in their own country. Also, the land is not being used to grow crops that would feed the poor living in that country.

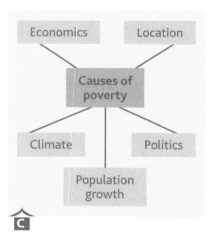

Activities

1 On this page and the previous three pages, there are five reasons discussed as to why countries are poor: location, politics, climate, population growth and economics. Put these reasons in order of importance. Explain your reasons for the ranking of the most and the least important reasons.

2 Which of these five causes of poverty do you think would be easiest to do something about? Explain what you think could be done.

3 'Rich countries should help poor countries by giving them food.' What do you think? Explain your opinion.

Research activity

When you next visit a supermarket spend a few minutes carefully looking at where the fruit and vegetables come from. Try to look at items that are not in season, e.g. strawberries in winter.

Summary

You should now be able to discuss why climate, population growth and economics are all reasons why some countries are poor.

Emergency aid and long-term aid

When a disaster such as an earthquake or flood strikes a region or country, the first few hours after the disaster are vital. It is then that lives can be saved, provided medical help is available. However, access to the disaster area can be difficult. An earthquake or floodwater may make roads impassable and it may be too dangerous to use an aircraft, even if one is available. As a result, valuable time is lost when it is most needed.

Objectives

Understand the difference between emergency aid and long-term aid.

Introduce the Muslim response to relief work.

Case study

2008 Pakistan earthquake

In October 2008, an earthquake caused devastation in and around Ziarat in Pakistan. Early estimates were that around 600 people had died and 2000 homes were destroyed. The first task was to rescue the living from the wreckage of buildings and treat their injuries and remove, identify and bury the dead.

Within 24 hours, international and Pakistani aid agencies were assisted by the Pakistani military in providing the survivors with medical relief and transport to the safety of the provincial capital of Quetta. They also provided tents, blankets and food to prevent there being more casualties. The World Health Organisation sent medical aid and supplies for 50,000 people to help the emergency relief effort.

A *The aftermath of the Pakistani earthquake*

However, as the situation changes, emergency aid such as food, clean water, shelter and medical supplies can be made available to the areas in most need. At this stage, saving lives is still the most important factor; success is judged by how many lives are saved or lost. Help may come from people in other parts of the affected country or it may be offered by those in other countries.

Once the immediate need is met and as many lives as possible have been saved, long-term aid begins. Temporary shelters need to be replaced by building permanent ones. Transport links, e.g. roads and railways, have to be re-established. Food needs to be grown rather than imported. Water supplies have to be made safe to drink. This may take years and works best if it is done by the local community, using their knowledge and expertise alongside that of the relief workers. The likelihood of such developments being sustainable, that is, lasting from year to year, is increased when local people are consulted and involved. This helps to make sure that they receive assistance that is acceptable and appropriate to their needs. They also develop their skills and a sense of pride in their achievements, and learn new skills that they can use again.

Ongoing work

Long-term aid does not only follow on from emergency aid. For example, many organisations work in LEDCs in an educational role. One of the most important educational tasks is teaching people about healthcare.

Key terms

Emergency aid: giving needy people short-term aid as a response to a crisis or disaster, e.g. food in times of famine or war.

Long-term aid: helping needy people to help themselves by providing the tools, education and funding for projects.

Activities

1 With a partner, write an action plan including a flow chart that could be produced in response to a serious earthquake.

2 How would you judge the success of your action plan?

In many parts of Africa, Acquired Immune Deficiency Syndrome (AIDS) is a major problem. Across the continent around 6000 people die of AIDS related illnesses every day. AIDS is an incurable condition caused by the Human Immunodeficiency Virus (HIV). HIV attacks the body's immune system although there are treatments that can control it. AIDS is the final stage of uncontrolled HIV when the immune system stops working and a life-threatening condition such as pneumonia can develop. More than 20 per cent of the adult population in some African countries have HIV, but have little knowledge about the disease or how they can prevent it. They also cannot afford treatments to control the effects of HIV.

Many organisations work to help this situation. Advice on methods of contraception, supported by the supply of contraceptive devices, is also vital if overpopulation is to be avoided.

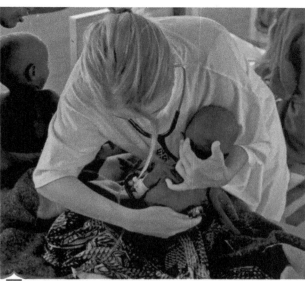

B *Relief worker giving healthcare*

Obviously providing healthcare for the sick is imperative, but training people to provide care in the future is equally important. In other words, the most effective long-term aid is focused on enabling the community to provide the care for themselves. This includes teaching children about basic healthcare as they are the next generation of adults.

Activities

3   Explain why long-term aid is focused on enabling the community to provide care for themselves.

4   What else do you think long-term aid workers should provide? Explain why. Be prepared to offer your ideas to the class.

Discussion activity

Apart from healthcare, what else do you think organisations should be *teaching* people in LEDCs? Discuss this with a partner and be prepared to share your ideas with the rest of the class.

A Muslim response

As can be seen from the following pages, Muslim relief organisations make a significant contribution to providing voluntary assistance to areas in need throughout the world. They do this regardless of nationality or religion. As with all ethical issues, Muslims consult the *Qur'an* for guidance. Here it makes very clear what their duties are:

Beliefs and teachings

Those who (in charity) spend of their goods by night and by day, in secret and in public, have their reward with their Lord: on them shall be no fear, nor shall they grieve.

Qur'an 2:274

Study tip

If writing about the work of a charity or relief organisation, specify whether it is providing emergency aid or long-term aid.

Summary

You should now understand the difference between emergency aid and long-term aid. You should also be able to evaluate the effectiveness of each type of aid.

2.6 The work of Muslim agencies in development and poverty relief

There are many Muslim relief organisations working to help the most disadvantaged people in the world. In addition, many Muslims support non–Muslim or secular organisations, e.g. UNICEF (the United Nations Children's Fund). They do this in the belief that the work these organisations do is not dependent on faith. If people are in need and someone is prepared to help them, then their own faith should not matter. Just because the local hospice or homelessness charity may be run by people who have a different or no religious faith does not mean Muslims will not support it.

Objectives

Know and understand the work of two Muslim relief organisations.

⚭ links

For more information on Muslim teachings on helping others, see pages 48–51.

Discussion activity 👥👥👥

'Muslims should only support charities that help other Muslims.' Do you agree? Discuss your thoughts about this with a partner and be prepared to share your ideas with the class.

Islamic Relief

Islamic Relief is an organisation dedicated to reducing the poverty and suffering of the world's poorest people. It started in Britain in 1984 and operates field offices in 13 countries. Some of these countries, including China, are countries where there are few Muslims. However, most are in countries where Muslims are in the majority. It helps to support relief activities in most of the poorest countries of the world. The organisation's inspiration is a passage from the *Qur'an*:

Beliefs and teachings

If any one saved a life, it would be as if he saved the life of the whole people.

Qur'an 5.32

A *The logo of Islamic Relief*

Research activity 🔍

Find out more about Islamic Relief at www.islamic-relief.com

This inspires Muslims from across the world to support Islamic Relief because they feel that Allah would want them to do so.

Islamic Relief is keen to empower people to lift themselves out of poverty by providing the opportunity and equipment to make it possible. It believes strongly that people should be able to take control of their own lives which gives them a sense of dignity and pride. It recognises the importance of education and training, health and nutrition, child welfare and the provision of safe drinking water. However, it also responds to situations where aid is needed in an emergency, e.g. earthquakes, droughts, floods and war. Once the immediate lifesaving needs are met, it assists in rebuilding such things as homes, roads and hospitals so life can quickly return to as near to normal as possible.

The Red Crescent

The Red Crescent is part of the same federation as the Red Cross. It carries out the same sort of relief work as the Red Cross but is based in Muslim countries. Its mission is to provide assistance without discrimination as to nationality, race, religious beliefs, class or political opinions. It supports the public authorities in their own country, who have local knowledge, expertise and access. Such knowledge, expertise and access allows the resources and personnel the Red Crescent provides to be targeted where it is needed and where it will be most effective.

B   *Muslim agencies provide for those in need*

The Red Crescent (and also the Red Cross) has seven principles:

- Humanity – it is prepared to help anybody wherever they are and without discrimination. It is also keen to protect human life and to ensure respect for every human being by promoting understanding, friendship, co-operation and peace.
- Impartiality – it is guided only by a person's needs and those in most distress are given priority, no matter who they are.
- Neutrality – in times of conflict or war, it does not take sides.
- Independence – although it follows the law of the country in which it is based, it is not an agency of that government.
- Voluntary service – emphasis is on relieving need not on personal gain.
- Unity – all societies in all countries have equal status and share equal responsibilities and duties.
- Universality – the Red Crescent society in any country has to be open to all.

Extension activity

Choose three of the seven principles of the Red Crescent that you think contribute most to their success as a relief organisation. Explain how each of your three principles contribute to this success.

Study tip

If you are asked about a Muslim relief organisation, you can use either of these. Make sure you name whichever one you choose.

Research activity

Find out about a specific project where either Islamic Relief or the Red Crescent has provided relief.

Activities

1   Choose either Islamic Relief or the Red Crescent and write a paragraph about its work.

2   'If any one saved a life, it would be as if he saved the life of the whole people' (*Qur'an* 5:32). Explain what you think this quotation means to a Muslim.

3   'No relief organisations should be allowed to identify with any religion.' Do you agree? Give reasons for your answer showing that you have thought about more than one point of view.

Summary

You should now know more about two Muslim relief organisations including the work they do and their reasons for doing it.

Muslim Aid

A *Logo of Muslim Aid*

Objectives

Know about and understand the role of Muslim Aid in providing relief aid.

Focus on the work of Muslim Aid in the Gaza conflict in 2009.

Muslim Aid was founded in London in 1985 when 23 community-based British Muslim organisations combined their work. This was in response to famine in Africa and other conflicts and disasters in Palestine, Afghanistan and Bangladesh. Since then it has responded to need throughout the world, wherever it is needed but, because of the level of need, mainly in LEDCs. By the end of 2008, it had established field offices in 14 countries including Sudan, Sri Lanka, Cambodia, Lebanon and India. These field offices enable it to provide relief and development programmes in over 70 countries.

As well as providing emergency relief when needed, Muslim Aid is based on the principle that in order to eradicate poverty, people require the means to improve their own lives. This involves working to provide education, clean water, healthcare and projects where people can learn to support themselves. Muslim Aid helps anyone in need, regardless of their race, religion or political opinions. It provides them with the basic necessities and helps them to become less dependent on aid organisations.

B *Location of Gaza*

Activities

What does the slogan 'Serving Humanity' tell you about Muslim Aid?

Muslim Aid works in partnership with other relief organisations including the Red Cross and Red Crescent. What do you think are the benefits of such partnerships?

The conflict in Gaza

G a narrow coastal strip of land which borders Israel, Egypt and Mediterranean Sea. It covers around 360 square kilometres (13 square miles) and has a population of around 1.5 million, main Muslims but with a minority of Christians as well. Gaza was part Palestine until 1948 when, after the Second World War, Israel was gi some of the territory by the United Nations to establish a Jewish te. Palestinians were governed by Israel between 1967 and 2005, lo g a proportion of their territory to Israel during this time.

Despite giving up control of Gaza in 2005, Israel retained control of the airspace over Gaza, its territorial waters and the border between themselves and Gaza. This allowed them to control everything that came into or out of the territory, including food and power. Some of this food was being supplied by relief organisations because of the poverty many Palestinians faced.

In 2006 the Hamas party, which opposed the control Israel had on Gaza, became the democratically elected government of Gaza. They felt that Israel was illegally occupying Palestine and many militant supporters of Hamas were prepared to fight against the Israelis.

In 2001, militants in Gaza started firing rockets into southern Israel. In the following seven years, they fired around 8600 rockets, killing 28 Israelis and wounding hundreds. On 27 December 2008, Israel launched air attacks. A few days later they followed this with a land offensive in an attempt to eliminate the Hamas militants responsible for the rocket attacks on Israel. Hundreds of civilians were killed including many children, in some cases whole families, whose homes were destroyed.

Once the conflict was over, buildings including hospitals and schools which were damaged or destroyed had to be rebuilt. Roads needed repairing to allow transport to function. Food and water supplies had to be restored. This is where organisations such as Muslim Aid became involved.

Muslim Aid had been delivering humanitarian and development assistance in Palestine for more than 20 years before the 2008–9 conflict. In 1998, 20 per cent of the people living in Gaza existed below the United Nations official poverty line. Ten years later this figure had grown to 64 per cent. Life for many had become a struggle to find enough food to ensure survival. This struggle was not helped by the Israeli blockade of their borders before the conflict.

After the conflict, Muslim Aid greatly increased their aid to Gaza by supplying food and medical supplies which were distributed by partner organisations within the territory. They also supported the Palestine Trauma Centre. This provided counselling for people left traumatised by the conflict, possibly having lost family members in the air and land assault by the Israeli army. Funding came from donations to a special appeal for £2 million launched by Muslim Aid once the desperate plight of many Palestinians living in Gaza became known.

 Muslim Aid brings supplies to Gaza, 2009

Activities

3 Describe the situation people in Gaza faced during and after the conflict in January 2009.

4 Write a paragraph asking people to support Muslim Aid's work in Gaza after the conflict.

2.8 Muslim organisations in the UK

In addition to providing relief in areas of need overseas, there are many Muslim organisations providing help where it is needed in Britain. For Muslims in need, the first point of contact is the family. This is usually effective. However, even though providing help is a duty in Islam, it is not always possible for the family to provide all the help that is needed. Young people may need help from their parents and elderly parents may be in need of help from their grown-up children. It is not always possible for families to provide this help.

Beliefs and teachings

We have enjoined on man kindness to his parents.

Qur'an 46:15

Most British Muslims in need of help that their family cannot provide will turn to their local mosque **community**. Here they will find a community prepared to give advice, education or if necessary material needs. The mosque is likely to serve as a community centre for local Muslims and the mosque committee shares responsibility for the well-being of Muslims in its locality.

Objectives

Understand how Muslim organisations provide help in the UK to relieve poverty and suffering.

Understand how the ideas of duty and community influence Muslims to help each other.

Key terms

Community: a group of people with a common link trying to make things better for each other.

A Birmingham Central Mosque

The Birmingham Central Mosque, as most others, offers many services to the local Muslim community. These range from family counselling and library services to evening school for children and community classes for adults. In addition, they offer help and support to people who are suffering though sickness, bereavement or the effects of poverty.

Beliefs and teachings

Give charity without delay, for it stands in the way of calamity.

Al-Tirmidhi, Hadith 589

The UK Islamic Mission

The UK Islamic Mission was founded as a registered charity in the early 1960s with the intention of serving the Muslim community and building bridges of understanding and mutual respect across faith communities. It aims to improve understanding of Islam by holding local, regional and national events to which anyone is invited.

Discussion activity

Do you think the family should be the first point of contact if a person is in need? Discuss this with a partner or small group.

B   *Muslim boys learning to read the Qur'an*

Young people are encouraged to take advantage of provision the Mission makes for their education and welfare. This includes Muslims learning more about their faith and non-Muslims learning about Islam in the hope that this will remove prejudice. The Mission also visits hospitals and prisons to offer assistance to those in need.

The UK Islamic Mission hopes that, by educating people about Islam, it will prevent future problems caused by lack of understanding and prejudice. The president of the UK Islamic Mission, Muhammad Sarfraz Madni, wrote:

> *Our doors are open to all, irrespective of individual belief, and we are always encouraging people to come forward and to join us in helping others – Muslims and non-Muslims alike.*
>
> *I hope and pray that God Almighty guides us all on His Righteous Way.*
>
> www.ukim.org

Activities

1   Explain the work of the UK Islamic Mission.

2   Do you think educating people about Islam may remove problems in the future? Give reasons for your opinion.

3   Helping others is a duty in Islam. Do you agree that helping others should be a duty for all people? Give reasons for your opinion.

Summary

You should now know about ways in which Muslims provide help for each other out of duty and a sense of community.

2.9 Zakah and Sadaqah

Zakah – compulsory giving

An important part of being a Muslim is to follow the Five Pillars. These five 'faith actions' help to reinforce the Ummah and show obedience to the will of Allah and unity between Muslims. The first pillar, shahadah, is the Muslim declaration of faith, to be repeated throughout one's life, that:

Beliefs and teachings

There is no God but Allah and Muhammad is the prophet of Allah.

It is within this context that the other four pillars should be seen. The third pillar is zakah – almsgiving (giving to charity). Muslims are required at the end of each lunar year, to give 2.5 per cent of their annual savings to help the poor. Cheating on this is seen as cheating on Allah so Muslims should take it seriously and give the correct amount without any attempt to make it less. The *Qur'an* makes it clear where this money should go:

Beliefs and teachings

Alms are for the poor and the needy, and those employed to administer the (funds); for those whose hearts have been (recently) reconciled (to Truth); for those in bondage and in debt; in the cause of Allah; and for the wayfarer: (thus is it) ordained by Allah, and Allah is full of knowledge and wisdom.

Qur'an 9:60

Furthermore, Muslims believe that all property belongs to Allah anyway. As a result the property a Muslim owns should not only be for their use, but also to help the poor because this is what Allah expects. Giving zakah brings blessings from Allah as it is seen as an act of worship. It is an act which pleases Allah as it contributes to making the world a better place. It also unites the rich and poor because the poor, in accepting zakah, are allowing the rich to receive Allah's blessing.

The word zakah literally means purity because giving zakah purifies a person from greed and selfishness. In addition the rest of a person's property is purified because the 2.5 per cent which is taken in zakah has been taken in accordance with Allah's instruction and not kept.

Muslims also believe that in creating hardship for themselves, as with fasting during Ramadan as well, they gain a greater insight into the hardship that others in the community face. In doing so, they are more able and willing to help those in trouble.

Objectives

Understand how Muslims provide relief for the poor including their giving through zakah and sadaqah.

Evaluate the effectiveness of zakah and sadaqah as ways of relieving poverty.

Key terms

Zakah: almsgiving (charity) of 2.5 per cent of wealth per year.

Sadaqah: voluntary almsgiving in addition to zakah.

∞ links

Look at pages 58–59 for more on the Five Pillars.

A *Saudi Arabian banknotes and coins*

Activities

1. Explain what zakah is.
2. Are there any other needy groups that you think should be added to the list in the *Qur'an* 9:60?
3. Explain why zakah is seen as an act of worship.
4. Do you think the poor should see their acceptance of zakah as helping the rich receive Allah's blessing? Explain the reasons for your answer.

Study tip

When writing about Muslims giving to charity, try to specify whether it is zakah or sadaqah you are writing about.

Sadaqah

Beliefs and teachings

So establish regular Prayer and give regular Charity; and obey the Messenger, that ye may receive mercy.

Qur'an 24:56

In addition to giving zakah every year, Muslims are also encouraged to give to good causes voluntarily. This is called sadaqah. It can take the form of money, time, prayer or talents and should be performed without boasting about it to others. It is said that it should be given so that the right hand of the giver does not know what the left hand is doing.

Because of the existence of sadaqah, major Muslim organisations such as Islamic Relief and Muslim Aid are able to launch specific charity appeals to respond to an urgent need. As a result they are successful in raising large amounts of money. Sadaqah also encourages people to offer more practical help as well. Sadaqah can also be given to non-Islamic charities like Comic Relief and Oxfam to enable them to carry out their good work. However, Muslims would want to satisfy themselves, before giving, that the projects they were supporting were in accordance with Muslim ethical principles.

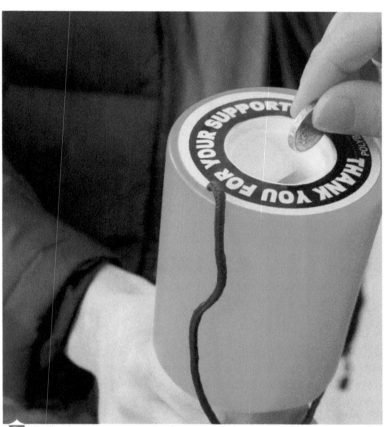

B   *Sadaqah encourages regular donations to charity*

Beliefs and teachings

So give what is due to kindred, the needy, and the wayfarer. That is best for those who seek the Countenance, of Allah, and it is they who will prosper.

Qur'an 30:38

Activities

5   Explain how sadaqah differs from zakah.

6   Can you think of any non-Islamic voluntary organisations that are not in accordance with Muslim ethical principles? If so, what are they?

Extension activity

In your opinion, which is best: giving to the poor as part of a religious duty or voluntary giving? Give your reasons.

Summary

You should now know and understand more about the ways in which Muslim communities provide for the poor, including zakah and sadaqah, and be able to evaluate their effectiveness.

Muslim attitudes to money and to giving to the poor

The gaining of money

Muslims see little wrong in the earning of money. Allah has given mankind the earth and it is right for us to explore and use the resources the earth provides, unless this exploration and use takes people's attention away from Allah:

Beliefs and teachings

In them is He glorified in the mornings and in the evenings... by men whom neither traffic nor merchandise can divert from the Remembrance of Allah.

Qur'an 24:36–7

It is perfectly acceptable for Muslims to own property and establish businesses; indeed it is Allah who makes it possible for people to be rich. Riches do not make a person superior to a poor person because having riches is a big responsibility.

Beliefs and teachings

He hath raised you in ranks, some above others: that He may try you in the gifts He hath given you.

Qur'an 6:165

However, Allah also imposes restrictions on how money can be gained. It is forbidden in Islam to make money out of money. Therefore usury (receiving interest on money) is not allowed; charging interest on a loan is also wrong. This is because it would mean the person making the loan is making a profit throughout the time the money is repaid and the poorer person repaying the loan is being exploited. In addition, for the same reason, gambling is not allowed, whether it is by taking part in a small raffle, playing the National Lottery or visiting a casino. There have been cases where Muslims have defied this rule by playing the National Lottery and winning large amounts. Their attempts to make up for their wrong by donating large sums of their winnings to their local community through the mosque have failed. The mosques refused to accept the money gained from gambling, even if it could have done some good.

For most Muslims the only way of honestly making money is by working for it. This is what is expected of them in order for them to support their family.

Beliefs and teachings

No-one eats better food than that which they have earned by their own labours.

Hadith

Man can have nothing but what he strives for.

Qur'an 53:39

Objectives

Know and understand Muslim attitudes to the gaining and use of money.

Evaluate these attitudes towards money.

Study tip

You can use or paraphrase quotations in your exam. You are not expected to give the references, but if you can remember where it comes from, e.g. the *Qur'an* or the *Hadith*, you should say so.

⬭links

See pages 134–135 for more on usury.

Research activity 🔍

Use the internet to research the story of Mukhtar Mohidin who won nearly £18 million on the National Lottery.

A *All forms of gambling are forbidden in Islam*

The use of money

Muslims are frequently reminded that money is most important for the good it can do. Bearing this in mind makes it relatively easy to decide how Muslims should use money. It should first be used to ensure the welfare of the family. Ensuring the family is properly cared for is a strong Muslim duty. As previously covered, 2.5 per cent of savings has to be paid in zakah every year. This is to help the poor and needy within the community. Sadaqah provides an opportunity to give more. Money should not be wasted, nor should it provide a life full of luxuries for some whilst others do not have enough to live:

> **Beliefs and teachings**
>
> Waste not by excess, for Allah loveth not the wasters.
>
> *Qur'an* 7:31

In addition, money should not be hoarded because money that is not used does no good. The *Qur'an* guards against this:

> **Beliefs and teachings**
>
> There are those who bury gold and silver and spend it not in the way of Allah. Announce unto them a most grievous penalty.
>
> *Qur'an* 9:34

⚭ links

See pages 48–49 for more information on zakah and sadaqah.

B   *Money should not be wasted on luxuries*

Summary

You should now know and understand Muslim attitudes to gaining and using money, particularly to help the poor and needy, and be able to evaluate some of these attitudes.

Wealth and poverty – summary

For the examination, you should now be able to:

- explain the Muslim ideas of duty to care for the poor and community, and relate them to the issues of:
  - the characteristics of Less Economically Developed Countries (LEDCs) and the causes of poverty
  - emergency aid and long-term aid
  - the work of Muslim organisations and agencies in world development and the relief of poverty
- know and understand the work of Muslim Aid and the principles on which its work is based, including relevant Muslim teachings
- know and understand ways in which Muslim communities in the UK work to relieve poverty and suffering including an understanding of zakah and sadaqah
- understand and evaluate Muslim attitudes to money and to giving to the poor and needy
- discuss topics from different points of view, using arguments and Muslim teachings.

Sample answer

1 Write an answer to the following examination question:

'Providing for your family is more important than providing for anybody else.'

Do you agree? Give reasons for your answer, showing that you have thought about more than one point of view. *(6 marks)*

2 Read the following sample answer:

> I agree completely with this quote. The family is much more important than anybody else. Everybody has a family so if every family looked after members of their own family, there would be no poverty. It says in the Hadith 'He who eats and drinks while his brother goes hungry is not one of us.' Even though this is written for Muslims, I think it applies to everybody. Allah provides for people in order that they should provide for their family. The elderly and the young cannot provide for themselves so who better than their family to provide for them?
>
> On the other hand, there are other people in need but perhaps their families should do more.

3 With a partner, discuss the sample answer. Do you think that there are other things that the student could have included in the answer?

4 What mark would you give this answer out of 6? Look at the mark scheme in the Introduction on page 7 (AO2). What are the reasons for the mark that you have given?

Practice questions

1   Look at the photograph and answer the following questions.

(a)   Explain **two** reasons why some countries are poor.   (*4 marks*)

Study tip Make sure you develop each of your reasons by giving added detail in explanation in order to earn all 4 marks.

(b)   Explain what Muslims believe about how their money should be spent.   (*4 marks*)

Study tip To gain full marks, you have to show that you have a clear knowledge and understanding of what Muslims believe. You have to develop your answer and/or analyse the beliefs.

(c)   'Helping the poor in LEDCs is the most important priority when deciding how to spend money.'
      Do you agree? Give reasons for your answer, showing that you have thought about more than one point of view.   (*6 marks*)

Study tip Think carefully of reasons why some people may agree with this quote and why some may disagree. Even though you are asked whether you agree, you must give another point of view as well.

3 Conflict and suffering

3.1 Purpose of life and justice

Introduction

This chapter explores Muslim views on conflict and suffering. It looks at how Muslim attitudes to conflict and peace are influenced by their beliefs. The Islamic teachings about the purpose of life, justice, reconciliation and peace are particularly important. These teachings help us to gain a better understanding of Muslim views on war, conflict and peace.

The purpose of life

A *The Qur'an guides Muslims throughout their life*

For a Muslim the purpose of life could be summed up in the simple phrase 'Obey God'. But what does that mean? To understand this fully we need to consider Muslim beliefs about the relationship between Allah and human beings. The word Islam in Arabic means 'submission, obedience and peace'. A Muslim is someone who has accepted the will of Allah. This has been revealed through the Holy *Qur'an* and Muhammad, the final prophet of Allah.

Throughout their life a Muslim should always be conscious of Allah and their responsibilities to Him. Having this awareness is known as Taqwa. A companion of the prophet compared Taqwa to walking through thorns in a forest and being careful not to tear one's clothing. As a Muslim lives their life they should be aware that all they do is for Allah and nothing exists except by His will. Obedience to God and avoiding temptation is essential because Allah knows everything.

The main purpose of life for a Muslim is worship (Ibadah). In Islam this means all acts of obedience to God as well as those required by the Five Pillars. This life is a test and when it is over the body will wait in the grave until the Day of Judgement. Everyone will be resurrected and Allah will fairly judge each person's actions and intentions during their life on earth. The permanent afterlife will be spent in either a wonderful paradise or eternal suffering in hell. For Muslims this life is meaningful and has purpose because it will determine where they spend the afterlife.

Beliefs and teachings

We shall test you with something of fear and hunger, some loss in goods or the fruits (of your toil), but give glad tidings to those who patiently preserve, who say, when afflicted with calamity; "To Allah we belong, and to Him is our return."

Qur'an 2:155–156

Objectives

Understand Muslim views on the purpose of life and justice.

Key terms

Justice: bringing about what is right, fair, according to the law or making up for a wrong that has been committed.

∞ links

Look up the definitions of 'Taqwa' and 'Ibadah' in the Glossary at the back of this book.

Activities

1. Describe what Muslims believe about the purpose of life.

2. 'Believing in an afterlife scares people into being good.' What do you think? Explain your opinion.

Discussion activity

Discuss in small groups what you think the main purposes of life are. Share your ideas with the rest of the class.

Extension activity

Construct a collage of images to show different ideas about the purpose of life. You could use newspapers, clip art or draw your ideas.

Justice

Beliefs and teachings

I have forbidden injustice for Myself and also forbidden it for you. So avoid being unjust to one another.

Hadith

We sent aforetime our apostles … with the Book and Balance (of Right and Wrong), that men may stand forth in justice.

Qur'an 57:25

Justice is the concept of right and fair actions based on just laws. Where there is justice there can be harmony and peace between people. In Islam justice is a supreme virtue. This means that it is a good moral quality that Muslims should embrace. The *Qur'an* makes clear that Allah expects people and nations to treat each other with respect, compassion and justice in all aspects of life. It makes clear that justice is a duty and injustice is against the will of Allah.

Achieving justice is not easy. Allah has given human beings the responsibility to bring about justice on earth. The *Qur'an* explains that Allah has sent his prophets and laws to help people understand how to achieve justice. These revelations give guidance on many aspects of justice. For example, treatment of the poor, widows, criminals and foreigners. Muslims are expected to unite against injustice and put things right. It is wrong to ignore injustice and the suffering of innocents. In the case of the law, victims have a right to be compensated by the wrongdoer.

If societies are to be fair and just, every individual has to contribute. Muslims believe that they must live their lives correctly. They follow the code of behaviour know as Shari'ah – the path. This gives guidelines that help Muslims judge behaviour and conduct. The laws help to determine what is halal (right action) or haram (wrong action). Muslims believe that if all people followed the will of Allah then justice would be achieved for everyone.

links

See Chapter 5 for more on Muslim beliefs about justice.

B *Justice is a key principle in Islam*

links

See pages 10–11 for more on Shari'ah.

Look up definitions of 'halal' and 'haram' in the Glossary.

Activities

3 Explain what is meant by the term justice.

4 How are Muslims guided by their faith to bring about justice?

5 'Justice is an impossible dream.' Do you agree? Give reasons for your answer, showing that you have thought about more than one point of view.

Research activity

Find out about the different types of Islamic laws and the way they are made. Present your findings in a leaflet 'A Guide to Islamic Law'.

Summary

You should now know and understand Muslim beliefs about the purpose of life and the concept of justice.

Study tip

Refer to Muslim beliefs about the purpose of life and justice when explaining Muslim views on the issues in this chapter, such as war, pacifism and protest.

3.2 Reconciliation and peace

Achieving harmony

The message of Islam is one of peace and harmony. Allah created everything and has entrusted mankind with the responsibility of living correctly in the world. He has provided guidance in the *Qur'an* and through his prophets to help people achieve this ideal. However, people have to decide to follow the correct path in life. Allah has given people a conscience and free will to choose for themselves. When a Muslim submits to the will of Allah, it is a positive action. It means that they must bring their desires, attitude and behaviour into harmony with Allah's will.

This principle also applies to Muslim societies. In order for there to be peace and harmony in society, it must be governed by rulers who act fairly. In some Islamic countries, religious and secular laws are the same. These societies are governed by Shari'ah law, which is taken from the *Qur'an*. They are also guided by the *Hadith* and the life of the Prophet as recorded in the Sunnah. A society governed in this way is called a theocracy.

In the modern world it is not always easy for Muslims to know what is right and wrong. The pressures of modern living often involve making decisions on things that have not been discussed in the sacred writings of the faith. This means that all Muslims, including rulers, sometimes need to interpret the teachings to know what is right. Allah expects people to use their reason and judgement. So Muslim scholars consult the *Qur'an* and interpret it to decide Islamic principles and create new laws.

Objectives

Understand Muslim views about reconciliation and peace.

Key terms

Peace: an absence of conflict which leads to happiness and harmony.

∞ links

The term 'Sunnah' is defined on page 8, or you can look it up in the Glossary at the back of this book.

Extension activity

Find out the meaning of the following words:

fard, mandub, mubah, makruh, haram.

Write a leaflet on Muslim rules of behaviour.

Discussion activity

Is it possible in the modern world to have a country which is ruled by God's laws (a theocracy)?

A *A modern theocracy: Saudi Arabia has declared the Qur'an as the constitution of the country and is governed by Islamic law*

Beliefs and teachings

Nor can goodness and evil be equal. Repel (evil) with what is better, then will he become thy friend.

Qur'an 41:34

Reconciliation

Human nature is such that it is inevitable that there will be disagreements. Not everyone will have the same opinion and sometimes there is a need for people to work together and compromise if harmony is to be achieved. The *Qur'an* teaches that when a wrong has been done, Muslims should look for ways that will help reconciliation, not pursue revenge.

Reconciliation means to bring about an end to disagreements between people and to establish friendly relationships. This means that the people involved have to accept that they have done wrong and be prepared to change. It also means that sometimes those who have been wronged have to be prepared to forgive those who have wronged them. Only when the parties involved are prepared to listen and compromise can reconciliation be made. The state of being reconciled would be one where there is harmony and peace.

Peace

One meaning of the word Islam is peace. But what is peace? Peace can be used to describe the relationship between people and their environment. In one way, peace describes the absence of intimidation, conflict and violence. In Islam the meaning of peace goes beyond this; for there to be peace there must also be no oppression, injustice, corruption or tyranny. Peace is a state of harmony which enables all people in society to be given the opportunity to achieve happiness and contentment. In the *Qur'an* it is made clear that it is God's will that people should establish peace in his world.

Peace can also refer to a person's state of being. Islam aims to create a peaceful society because not only is this Allah's will, but it is necessary for individuals to grow spiritually and morally. Muslims often greet each other with a handshake and the phrase Salamu Alaykum which means 'peace be upon you'. This is also said to conclude the daily prayers when a Muslim turns to each side. In this way, Muslims are reminded of the ideal of peace constantly throughout their daily lives.

Discussion activity

"It is impossible to always forgive wrong doing." Discuss this statement in small groups. Share your ideas with the rest of the class.

B   *Peace is not only absence of war*

Beliefs and teachings

Allah doth call to the Home of Peace: He doth guide whom He pleaseth to a way that is straight.

Qur'an 10:25

Activities

1. Explain **two** ways Islam teaches that peace and harmony can be achieved.
2. What does reconciliation mean?
3. 'It is impossible to forgive some actions.' What do you think? Explain your opinion.
4. How can Muslims practise peace in their daily lives?
5. 'It is impossible to have peace when people have different beliefs.' How far do you agree? Give reasons for your answer showing that you have thought about more than one point of view.

links

Learn more about Muslim views on reconciliation and peace on pages 72–73.

Study tip

Remember that when you are asked about peace, you need to include more than simply the absence of conflict or war.

Summary

You should now know and understand Muslim views on reconciliation and peace.

3.3 Greater jihad

Jihad

The term jihad is often thought to mean only holy war, but its true meaning is much broader than that. In Islam the term jihad means to 'strive or struggle'. It is used on many occasions in the *Qur'an* to describe the idea of striving in the path of Allah. It is a duty for Muslims to struggle to improve themselves and the societies in which they live. All Muslims must endeavour to resist temptation and the desire to act selfishly. They should make every effort to live as Allah has instructed, to be conscientious in their faith and to do all they can for the good of others. The Prophet described this as the greater jihad.

Objectives

Understand the terms jihad and greater jihad.

Key terms

Jihad: a struggle against evil. This may be personal or collective.

Beliefs and teachings

Muhammad said: 'one who carries out jihad is he who strives against himself so he may obey Allah.'

Hadith

Greater jihad

For Muslims the greater jihad is the foundation of their lives. The greater jihad is the personal struggle of every Muslim to live their lives as Allah has willed it for them. The Five Pillars of Islam are one way in which Muslims are brought closer to Allah by performing them. They are reminded in the shahadah and salah to put God's will first every day of their life. The giving of zakah reminds them that what they have is because Allah wills it and that they have a duty to care for others. In performing sawm, Muslims learn to empathise with the poor and the discipline of the fast helps them develop the qualities to overcome temptation. The hajj is the most spiritual journey a Muslim will make in their lives. For ten days they leave behind all worldly concerns and humble themselves to God's will.

Beliefs and teachings

This is My (Allah's) way, leading straight: Follow it: Follow not (other) paths.

Qur'an 6:153

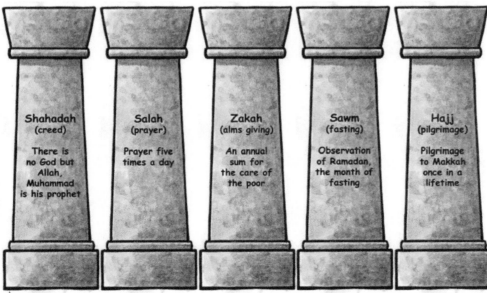

A *The Five Pillars of Islam*

Shahadah (creed)	Salah (prayer)	Zakah (alms giving)	Sawm (fasting)	Hajj (pilgrimage)
There is no God but Allah, Muhammad is his prophet	Prayer five times a day	An annual sum for the care of the poor	Observation of Ramadan, the month of fasting	Pilgrimage to Makkah once in a lifetime

Extension activity

Find out about the Muslim pilgrimage to Makkah. Write a diary for a pilgrim explaining the difficulties they experienced completing the hajj and how they feel this will help them in their everyday lives.

It is not easy to maintain such disciplines in the modern world. The pressures of work, family life and perhaps living in a non-Muslim society can make it difficult to fulfil these demands. Muslims know that Allah sees all that they do and the intentions in their heart. They understand that the difficulties they encounter are part of life. They also understand that the true test of their character is the effort they make to deal with these difficulties. Muslims are expected to develop positive qualities in their character such as compassion, honesty and generosity. This means learning to overcome negative attitudes such as anger, jealousy or greed.

There are many other ways that a Muslim may engage with the greater jihad. Some Muslims choose to learn the *Qur'an* by heart. This takes great patience and perseverance to accomplish. It is important to do this. It ensures that Allah's revelation will never be lost as millions of Muslims around the world are able to recite the entire *Qur'an*. Someone who is able to do so is called Hafiz meaning 'guardian'. Others may choose to contribute to the community in other ways such as social service, running the madrassah (Mosque school) or other voluntary work. In some cases they may need to participate in a lesser jihad.

B   *Muslim aid workers*

Beliefs and teachings

God does not accept belief if it is not expressed in deeds; and He does not accept deeds unless they are within your faith.

Hadith

A man with parents once asked the prophet if he should join the jihad. The prophet replied that he should, 'strive by serving them!'

Sunnah

links

Learn more about lesser jihad on pages 60–61.

Activities

1   What does the word jihad mean?
2   What are the Five Pillars of Islam? What difficulties might a Muslim have keeping them in a non-Muslim society?
3   Explain **two** ways that a Muslim could engage with the greater jihad.
4   'Keeping the Five Pillars of Islam is the most important thing in life for a Muslim.' Do you agree? Give reasons for your answer showing that you have thought about more than one point of view.

Research activity

Find out about the work of the Red Crescent to help victims of conflict.

Study tip

Remember to use examples to help you explain beliefs in longer answer questions.

Summary

You should now know what the word jihad means and understand the Muslim concept of greater jihad.

3.4 Lesser jihad

Lesser jihad

Lesser jihad means 'holy war'. It is known as Jihad as-sayf, the jihad of the sword. This involves armed combat against non-Muslim aggressors. It is the only form of war that Islam permits and there are strict rules covering its conduct. It applies to the relationships between nations. If a non-Muslim nation attacks Islam and all forms of diplomacy fail to resolve the problem, then it is the duty of Muslims to fight in self-defence and to gain justice for the oppressed. A soldier fighting in a war is called a mujahid; mujahideen is the plural.

Beliefs and teachings

To those against whom war is made, permission is given to fight because they are wronged.

Qur'an 22:39

A *A group of mujahideen*

When is a holy war allowed?

During the time of the Prophet there were many armed conflicts. These took place at a time when fighting between various tribes was commonplace. It was necessary for Muslims to fight in order to defend themselves. The *Qur'an* includes a number of teachings that make clear that it is right or just to fight in some situations. The most important aim of this jihad is to defend Islam and the rights of Muslims.

A holy war cannot be declared to force people to convert to the religion of Islam. It cannot be used to take over other countries or to take their land for financial gain. As with all actions in life, a holy war must be for Allah and never for a leader to demonstrate their power. All efforts must have been made to achieve peace; war must be a last resort.

What are the rules of a holy war?

A holy war can only be called by a fair spiritual leader. When this happens Muslims have a duty to respond. The Prophet said that half of the men from each village should fight; some should remain to defend the women, children, elderly and sick. Those whose families could not survive without them should stay. However, if a town was attacked, everyone living there should fight back. Soldiers on the battlefield should not run away because this makes it harder for their brothers. Any Muslim who dies in the defence of Islam will be welcomed into paradise.

Reasons for military jihad
- Self-defence
- Defence of Muslim faith and territory
- Defence of Muslim rights to worship and practise their faith
- Removal of oppressive rulers
- Punishment of enemies who break peace agreements
- To correct an injustice

Study tip

If you are asked to explain the rules of a holy war, you need to say why these points are important and not just bullet point them.

Make ready your strength to the utmost of your power, including steeds of war, to strike terror into (the hearts of) the enemies.

Qur'an 8:60

Allah loves those who fight in His cause.

Qur'an 61:4

Hate your enemy mildly, for one day he may become your friend.

Hadith

Conduct during a war

- War can only start when the enemy attacks
- Civilians should not be harmed or mistreated
- Crops and animals should not be destroyed
- Holy buildings and residential areas should not be damaged
- Prisoners of war must be treated well
- War must end when the enemy wants peace
- Human rights must be restored

B *The after-effects of a bombing raid*

Activities

1. What is meant by the term 'lesser jihad'?
2. Explain why Muslims must be prepared to fight in a war.
3. Explain the rules of a holy war.
4. What do the quotations on this page tell us about Muslim attitudes to war?
5. Look at Photo **B**. Why does it go against the teachings of Islam about the conduct of war?
6. 'It is impossible to have a Holy War; innocent people will always be mistreated.' What do you think? Give reasons for your opinion.

Extension activities

1. Explain how the teachings of the purpose of life, justice, reconciliation and peace influence Muslim attitudes to war.
2. Explain how the Islamic rules of conduct during a war might help to minimise suffering.

Summary

You should now know and understand the Muslim teachings of lesser jihad.

3.5 Disarmament and pacifism

What is disarmament?

Disarmament means to 'give up arms', meaning weapons. This can be multilateral disarmament which involves a number of countries all agreeing to reduce or abolish certain weapons. This requires the parties involved to reach agreements between them about the actions they will take and the timescale in which it will take place. It is often an important aspect of reconciliation treaties. Unilateral disarmament occurs when the government of one country decides to abolish certain weapons by their own choice. The country does not wait for other nations to do the same but will make their own decision without involving any other nations.

A *The Disarmament sculpture outside the United Nations*

In the modern world the 'arms race' has led to some countries stockpiling weapons of mass destruction (WMDs). These include nuclear and biological weapons that are capable of killing thousands and destroying vast areas with a single missile. Many people believe that the world will never be at peace until countries all agree to give up these frightening weapons. As well as achieving peace this would enable the billions of dollars spent worldwide on such weapons to be used on more worthwhile causes such as abolishing poverty.

Muslim attitudes to disarmament

If the world was perfect as Allah intended, then no weapons would ever be needed. Human selfishness and injustice has meant that it is sometimes necessary to take up arms in self-defence. Muslims have a duty to defend Islam and to fight against tyranny, oppression and injustice. This means that disarmament can only be achieved in an atmosphere of reconciliation. Many Muslim countries have participated in United Nations conferences on issues related to disarmament and

Objectives

Understand Muslim attitudes to disarmament and pacifism.

Key terms

Disarmament: when a country gets rid of its weapons.

Pacifism: the belief that it is unacceptable to take part in war and any other form of violence.

Research activity

Find out more about UN Disarmament at http://disarmament.un.org/treatystatus.nsf

Extension activity

1 Look at photo A of the Disarmament sculpture outside the United Nations building. Design your own symbol for disarmament and explain it to the rest of the class.

weapons control. They have also signed treaties and conventions agreeing to the reduction and abolition of certain weapons. For example, the UN convention on land mines has been signed by a number of Muslim nations including Algeria, Jordan and Qatar.

Beliefs and teachings

Make peace between them with justice, and be fair; For Allah loves those who are fair and just.

Qur'an 49:9

Fighting is prescribed for you, and you dislike it.

Qur'an 2:216

■ Pacifism and Islam

Pacifism is the belief that violence and war are wrong. Pacifists will not fight in a war; they believe that killing people in war is wrong and that there are better ways to resolve conflicts between people and nations. They believe in using non-violent action to achieve peace and the resolution of problems. Pacifism is not a religious belief, but a moral principle that many religious believers have adopted. It is connected with religious teachings such as the sanctity of human life. Pacifists object to war and violence because it leads to the destruction of life and encourages brutality and injustice.

Islam makes clear that it is wrong to allow injustice to continue and that when faced with an aggressor, it is right to defend oneself. Lesser jihad is a duty for Muslims and is sometimes believed to be necessary. Pacifism does not fit easily with these beliefs. However, it is important to remember that Islam is a faith based on the principles of peace and tolerance. Disputes should be resolved amicably and justice established for all. It would therefore be fair to say that Islam would see the ideals of pacifism as just, but that it is not always right to refuse to fight.

B *Khan Abdul Ghaffar Khan, a Muslim pacifist*

Beliefs and teachings

And why should you not fight in the cause of Allah and of those who, being weak, are ill-treated and oppressed?

Qur'an 4:75

And the hypocrites were told: 'Come, fight in the way of Allah, or at least drive the foe from your city.' They said: 'Had we known how to fight, we should certainly have followed you.' They were that day nearer to Unbelief than to Faith.

Qur'an 3:167

■ What is terrorism?

To be in terror is to be in complete fear. Terrorism is the term used to describe acts of violence carried out with the intention of intimidating and causing fear in the victims. A terrorist is anyone who plans and carries out such attacks. Most people would agree with the United Nations who have declared that acts of terrorism are criminal activities and are a violation of human rights.

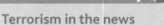
A   A car bomb explodes

Terrorism usually involves attacks that are deliberately targeted against civilians. The actions of the terrorists are intended to cause fear, injury and destruction. Attacks have included bombings, kidnapping, assassinations, hijacking and poisoning.

Terrorist groups tend to be made up of individuals with extreme and militant views. These can be related to political, ethical or religious beliefs. There are terrorist groups associated with political struggles across the world and environmental, animal rights and anti-abortion groups who use terrorist tactics to publicise their cause. There are also examples of terrorist groups like Al Qaeda, who claim to be fighting a holy war. The actions of terrorist groups are a consequence of a firm belief that what they are fighting for is right and that there is no alternative other than to use violence. Some individuals are prepared to die for their cause and the news frequently includes stories of suicide bombers attacking civilian areas. There are those that would argue that these people are not terrorists but 'freedom fighters'. They see their actions as battles within a war, rather than as criminal activity.

Case study

European day for the victims of terrorism

On 11 March 2005 the European Community held its first day of remembrance for the victims of terrorism. This is now an annual event and the date chosen is the anniversary of the terrorist attacks in Madrid in 2004. The day is held to show support for all those who have suffered the effects of terrorist actions. It is a day to remember those who have lost their lives and to affirm the European Union's commitment to democracy and human rights. It is marked with acts of commemoration throughout Europe.

B   The memorial to the victims of the terrorist attacks in Madrid in 2004

Discussion activity

2   Read the case study. What do you think? Is it a good idea to have a memorial day of this kind? What kind of activities would you suggest to mark the occasion? Discuss your opinions with a partner or in a small group.

⚭ links

Find out more about the European Network of Victims of Terrorism at: www.giornatadellamemoria.net

Muslim views about terrorism

In recent years the highly publicised activities of extreme fundamentalists claiming their actions are based on Islamic teaching has resulted in the misrepresentation of Islam, particularly in the West. The *Qur'an* makes clear that violence is wrong and against the will of Allah. War is only justified in self-defence. The rules of the lesser jihad include defence of civilians and property. To incite fear in innocent people, randomly destroy property and take life is not only an act of cowardice, but strictly forbidden. Islam is based on principles of peace, justice and freedom. Most Muslims would consider acts of terrorism to be against Islamic law. The *Qur'an* makes clear that Muslims have a duty to establish peace on earth and actions that are against this are condemned.

C   *11 September 2001, Al Qaeda attacks in New York cause outrage across the world*

Beliefs and teachings

Let there be no compulsion in religion.

Qur'an 2:256

If any one slew a person – unless it be for murder or spreading mischief in the land – it would be as if he slew the whole people.

Qur'an 5:32

Do not kill yourselves, for verily Allah has been to you most merciful! If any do that in rancour and injustice, soon shall we cast them into the fire.

Qur'an 4:29–30

Do not take life which Allah has made sacred.

Qur'an 17:33

Activities

4   Explain Muslim attitudes to terrorism. Refer to beliefs and teachings in your answer.

5   'Peace is an impossible dream.' What do you think? Explain your opinion.

Study tip

Using quotations in longer answer questions will improve your answer. Don't worry if you can't remember the exact wording. Summarising as nearly as possible is acceptable.

Summary

You should now know and understand Muslim beliefs about terrorism and Muslim attitudes to terrorists.

Nuclear war and proliferation

Nuclear war and proliferation

A **nuclear war** is one in which nuclear weapons are used. The bombing of the Japanese cities of Hiroshima and Nagasaki, by the US in the Second World War, is the only example. The horrific and devastating effects of the attack brought about an immediate surrender. These weapons are classified as weapons of mass destruction (WMDs) because they are capable of killing and maiming thousands of people with a single warhead. They also have a devastating effect on the landscape and the radiation from the mushroom cloud can contaminate areas miles from the site of the attack.

Initially only a few countries had a nuclear capability, notably the US, the USSR and Britain. However, as communications and technologies have developed, a number of other countries now have nuclear weapons. Despite United Nations' treaties to reduce these weapons, there is still a growing number of nuclear weapons in more places around the world. This is known as **nuclear proliferation**.

Research activity 🔍

Find out about the work of the Campaign for Nuclear Disarmament (CND). Working in a small group, make a poster showing the main aims and activities of the organisation.

The nuclear disarmament debate

Since the Second World War there has been an undeclared understanding that the destructive force of nuclear weapons is such that they can never be used. This raises the question of why countries continue to have and develop them. The debate has become more about whether countries should have nuclear weapons in order to deter other countries from attacking them.

A *A nuclear mushroom cloud*

B *Protest against nuclear weapons*

C *Map of Japan*

I am a British Muslim and I do not think that we should get rid of our nuclear weapons. We need them to be a deterrent to stop other countries attacking us. The deterrent must work because they have not been used since the last world war. Having these weapons means that no one will use them against us, which means that we can live in peace. These weapons have been developed now and are part of modern warfare. There is no point just giving up that research. Britain needs to have a nuclear capability to be able to have an equal say when the United Nations makes treaties for the reduction in nuclear arms.

I am a Muslim living in Qatar and I am happy that our country does not have nuclear weapons. It is wrong to spend so much money on something that could destroy the world when millions of people are living in poverty. It can never be right to use weapons that would kill thousands of innocent people and if they are never to be used, it would be a great waste of money. Countries that have these weapons are just encouraging others to develop them when we should be working to develop policies of peace for the world. It is wrong to say that peace can only be achieved by having something which just causes fear.

 Differing views on the nuclear deterrent

What does Islam say about nuclear weapons?

There are no direct references to nuclear warfare in Muslim sacred writings because this is a modern issue. However, there is a great deal that can be applied. Allah created the world and Muslims have a duty to care and strive for peace. Muslims believe all life is sacred and that even in war the aim is defence and ultimately peace. It would therefore be wrong to use nuclear weapons. Their destructive effects are such that they cannot be in keeping with the principles of lesser jihad. However, in world talks Islamic nations have taken different positions on the issues. Iran has signed the UN nuclear non-proliferation treaty, whilst Pakistan has a nuclear weapons capability.

Discussion activity

Organise a class debate on this topic: 'Should Britain give up its nuclear weapons?'

Activities

1 Why are nuclear weapons called weapons of mass destruction?
2 What is meant by the following terms?
a nuclear proliferation
b nuclear disarmament
3 Explain **three** reasons for and **three** reasons against nuclear disarmament.
4 'The use of nuclear weapons in a war could never be justified.' What do you think? Explain your opinion.
5 Explain differing Muslim attitudes to nuclear weapons as a deterrent.
6 'Nuclear weapons could never be used in a holy war.' What do you think? Explain your opinion.

Beliefs and teachings

Make not your own hand contribute to your destruction.

Qur'an 2:195

Study tip

Some AO2 questions will ask you to explain your opinion as you can see in Activity 4 and Activity 6. Remember that you must use reasons to do this. A reason is something that has evidence to support the point and not just a personal feeling about something.

Summary

You should now know and understand about Muslim views on nuclear war and proliferation and be able to discuss advantages and disadvantages of countries holding nuclear weapons.

3.8 Protest

Why protest?

A **protest** is any action an individual or group may take to draw attention to an issue or cause in which they believe. Protests usually arise when people feel an injustice has occurred. People can protest against injustice in many different ways. These range from writing letters, boycotting products and joining protest groups to even breaking the law and going to prison. People may decide on some kind of public protest because they feel they have no other way to make their voices heard. It is a way to attract media attention and make other people aware of the issue. Protesters may think that it is right to stand up for what they believe. Sometimes people believe that it is the only way to bring about change or correct something that is wrong.

When people are first made aware of an injustice, if they feel strongly about the matter, they will consider what action to take. Non-violent protests involve methods of protesting that do not cause harm to others or damage to property. These can be simple actions such as signing a petition, writing to your MP or opting not to buy the goods and services of a particular company. Other forms of non-violent protest may involve more direct action: marches, sit-ins (occupying a building or space), refusing to work such as strike action or causing disruption such as blocking roads. These actions can be very frustrating for individuals and companies who are affected by the protests. However, none of these is intended to cause any direct harm to others.

Some protesters feel that non-violent actions such as these are not enough. They believe that the only way their concerns will be listened to is if they use more extreme forms of protest. This can include methods that are intended to intimidate others and force change. Change may be achieved because public opinion changes and supports the protest. On the other hand, change may be achieved as a result of fear, frustration or simply because the pressures caused by the protesters make it impossible to continue. There are many examples of protests, both violent and non-violent, that have achieved their goal and brought about change.

A Muslim protest march

Extension activity

1 Using the internet, find out more about a particular protest or campaign that Muslims have been involved in which would be supported by principles in the *Qur'an*.

B *Forms of protest*

Discussion activity

What forms of protest can you see in Picture **B**? Are they violent or non-violent? What methods of protest do you think are acceptable? Does it depend on what the protest is about?

Extension activities

2 Which forms of protest do you think would be most effective? Explain your answer.

3 A Muslim should only ever use non-violent forms of protest. What do you think? Explain your opinion.

■ Muslim attitudes to protest

Islam teaches that Muslims have a duty to do what they can to achieve peace and justice in the world. If a Muslim sees something that is clearly against the will of Allah and is unjust, it would be wrong to simply ignore this. There are therefore occasions when it is right to protest and this may form part of a Muslim's personal jihad, to strive against what is wrong. Most Muslims would agree that non-violent protest is acceptable. However, the use of violence cannot be justified unless the protesters' actions are in self-defence.

○○links

Learn more about Muslims and protest in the case study on pages 70–71.

Beliefs and teachings

Fight them until there is no more oppression and there prevail justice.

Qur'an 2:193

The prophet was asked what kind of jihad is better. He replied, 'A word of truth in front of an oppressive ruler.'

Sunnah

Activities

1 Why is it sometimes necessary for people to protest?

2 Describe **three** methods of non-violent protest.

3 Explain why it is acceptable for a Muslim to take part in a protest.

4 'Muslims should never use violence to protest.' What do you think? Explain your opinion.

Summary

You should now know about different forms of protest and Muslim attitudes to them.

Introduction

We have seen that Muslims have a responsibility to speak out against injustice and oppression. Violence is not permitted unless it is in self-defence. Non-violent protest is one way that Muslims can strive for peace and justice when there are wrongs that need correcting. There have been a number of protests in the UK by the Muslim community. These have included marches against racism and Islamophobia (fear of Islam) and the wars in the Persian Gulf and Middle East. Individual Muslims have also taken part in protests relating to issues about which their conscience tells them they should speak out. Islam teaches that it is right to stand up for what you believe in and protesting against what a Muslim considers to be wrong, is a personal jihad.

Objectives

Examine an example of Muslim protest.

Beliefs and teachings

If you see an evil action change it with your hand, or your tongue, or your heart.

Hadith

Defending the faith

On 30 September 2005 a Danish newspaper published a series of cartoons depicting the Prophet Muhammad and making a joke out of aspects of Islamic teachings and beliefs. Danish Muslims objected to the publications and held peaceful protests to raise awareness of the newspaper's actions. The news of this controversy quickly spread around the world and the cartoons were reprinted in newspapers in more than 50 other countries.

Muslims across the world were outraged. The teaching of Islam strictly forbids the drawing of the Prophet and the caricatures were considered offensive to Islam. Muslims felt the images were racist and blasphemous and many non-Muslims who joined the protests agreed with them. Many of these protests were peaceful. Men, women and children marched peacefully together in cities around the world carrying placards and listening to speeches by leaders. They protested outside Danish embassies and demanded respect and tolerance of people's beliefs. Their view was that the images represented an abuse of freedom of speech.

Other protestors were more violent in their actions. Banners and chants called for the death of the cartoonists and bomb threats were made. Protestors were killed in some rioting that took place in Pakistan. Danish embassies in some countries were fire bombed and Danish flags were burned. The protests led to considerable diplomatic activity, with Arab nations petitioning the Danish government to take action. A number of Muslim groups filed a petition with the Danish police claiming that the newspaper's action was a crime since it breached the Danish blasphemy laws.

A *Muslim protestors*

Beliefs and teachings

Allah holds back His punishment from him who has held back his anger.

Hadith

In January 2006 the Danish newspaper published an apology to Muslims for the offence they had caused. The Danish prime minister described the whole episode as the worst international crisis Denmark had endured since the war. The boycott of Danish products around the world had cost Danish businesses in the region of 170 million dollars. Around the world 139 people had lost their lives during the protests. In the UK, four young British Muslims were imprisoned for inciting terrorism as a consequence of their conduct during a protest march in London.

B *Protestors burn the Danish flag*

The case study illustrates how deeply people can be offended when their faith is attacked. Most of the protests that took place were conducted peacefully by Muslims who felt they had a duty to respond to such insults. These people did not have some hidden agenda, but were genuinely distressed that their beliefs could be treated with such indifference and insensitivity. Across the world non-Muslims also expressed their support for the rights of people to not have their faith ridiculed. It raises many questions about the freedom of expression versus the need for censorship. Should action be taken to protect religious beliefs from such publications? What do you think?

Activities

1. Explain different Muslim attitudes to protest.
2. Describe the forms of protests Muslims used in this case study.
3. With reference to this case study: 'Muslims were right to protest.' What do you think? Explain your opinion.
4. What do you think are the most effective ways to protest? Explain your choices.

Discussion activity

Does 'freedom of speech' mean that people should be allowed to say anything they want, even if it is offensive?

Research activity

Find out about another example of a Muslim protest. Present your findings to the rest of the class. Remember to explain the forms of protest used and the reasons for the protest.

Summary

You should now know different ways that Muslims have protested and understand the effects of these protests.

Study tip

You will not have to write about a case study in the exam, but it will be useful to help you exaplin Muslim attitudes to protest.

Reconciliation

For people and societies to thrive and live in peace, there needs to be an atmosphere of mutual respect and tolerance. Islam teaches that all people are created equal and that diversity between groups should not stand in the way of friendly relationships. Muslims have a duty to strive for peace in the world. The *Qur'an* teaches that exploitation and domination are wrong. The vision of Islam is a world of peace where Muslims and non-Muslims work together for justice.

Beliefs and teachings

Do not create disorder in the world after it has been set in order.

Qur'an 7:57

In the modern world Muslim nations fully participate in world affairs. Organisations such as the United Nations are a positive way for countries to work together. For Muslims, it is a duty to bring about peaceful settlements when there are disputes between people. Through discussion and negotiation many Muslim countries have signed treaties and covenants with other nations on issues such as the environment, human rights and fair trade. This is one way in which nations can reconcile their different views.

A *Muslim nations participate in world affairs at the UN*

Peace is essential to building fair and just societies. This means that it is sometimes necessary to make personal sacrifices and accept the demands of others. In the early days of Islam the Prophet agreed to the Hudaiybiya Treaty. The no-war agreement was made by accepting all of the demands of the Quraish, the dominant tribe in Mekkah at the time Islam began, including not making the hajj that year. The *Hadith* make reference to the Prophet's insistence that people should feel safe in the presence of a Muslim and that a true believer would not make mischief for his neighbour.

Objectives

Understand Muslims views on reconciliation.

Examine some examples of reconciliation.

Key terms

Reconciliation: when two people or groups of people who have disagreed or fought with each other make up.

Research activity

Find out more about the work of the UN to bring about peace between the nations.

Red Crescent in Iraq

Following the war in Iraq the Red Crescent has been active in helping to support the thousands of families left homeless and in desperate need. The agency has been the main source for the distribution of emergency supplies of food, medicines and other necessities. Working in dangerous conditions and under threat of kidnap, the volunteers have maintained their commitment to the people and the ideals of the International Red Cross and Red Crescent movement. They have given hope to those suffering the effects of war and are helping them to rebuild their lives.

B   *Red Crescent aid workers collect emergency supplies*

Case study

Reconciliation after conflict

Within the rules of the lesser jihad there is consideration given to the need for reconciliation. A war may only be waged in self-defence and the rules state that peace must be achieved. If the enemy wants to make peace there must be an immediate end to hostilities. During the conduct of the war, prisoners must be treated respectfully. In his final sermon, the Prophet said that prisoners should be fed and clothed and that ill treatment was unacceptable. Innocent women and children should not be harmed and towns should not be destroyed. This means that after the conflict, people will be able to get on with their lives.

Beliefs and teachings

Hate your enemy mildly, one day he may become your friend.

Hadith

Once the enemy has been defeated the principle of mercy should be applied. In reaching a peace agreement there must be no exploitation; the land and resources of another nation should not be stolen. Prisoners of war should be returned unharmed and never executed. In the modern world the Red Crescent is the Islamic partner of the Red Cross movement. It works in many parts of the world to provide aid for those suffering from the effects of conflict.

Discussion activity

Read the case study. Why do you think some people continue to be volunteers when their own lives are put in danger? Discuss this with a partner or in a small group.

∞ links

Find out more about the work of the Red Crescent on pages 42–43 or at **www.ifrc.org**

Activities

1   Why is reconciliation important to Muslims?
2   Why do Muslims think it is important to participate in world affairs?
3   Explain how the rules of lesser jihad would make reconciliation after a war easier to achieve.
4   'Justice is more important than reconciliation.' What do you think? Explain your opinion.

Extension activity

Look at some examples of charity appeals in newspapers. Now write one for the Red Crescent.

Summary

You should now know about Muslim views on reconciliation and consider some ways in which Muslims practise reconciliation.

Study tip

Make sure you learn the meaning of key terms for each topic.

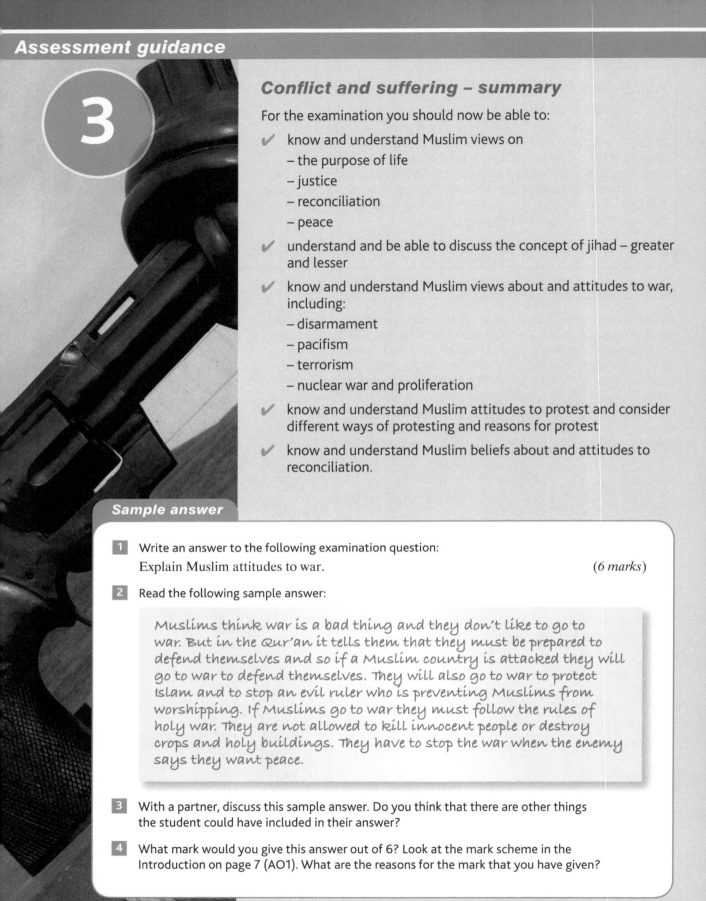

3

Conflict and suffering – summary

For the examination you should now be able to:

✔ know and understand Muslim views on
  – the purpose of life
  – justice
  – reconciliation
  – peace

✔ understand and be able to discuss the concept of jihad – greater and lesser

✔ know and understand Muslim views about and attitudes to war, including:
  – disarmament
  – pacifism
  – terrorism
  – nuclear war and proliferation

✔ know and understand Muslim attitudes to protest and consider different ways of protesting and reasons for protest

✔ know and understand Muslim beliefs about and attitudes to reconciliation.

Sample answer

1 Write an answer to the following examination question:
Explain Muslim attitudes to war. (*6 marks*)

2 Read the following sample answer:

> Muslims think war is a bad thing and they don't like to go to war. But in the Qur'an it tells them that they must be prepared to defend themselves and so if a Muslim country is attacked they will go to war to defend themselves. They will also go to war to protect Islam and to stop an evil ruler who is preventing Muslims from worshipping. If Muslims go to war they must follow the rules of holy war. They are not allowed to kill innocent people or destroy crops and holy buildings. They have to stop the war when the enemy says they want peace.

3 With a partner, discuss this sample answer. Do you think that there are other things the student could have included in their answer?

4 What mark would you give this answer out of 6? Look at the mark scheme in the Introduction on page 7 (AO1). What are the reasons for the mark that you have given?

Practice questions

1   Look at the photograph and answer the following questions.

(a)   Explain briefly what is meant by the term 'greater jihad'.   *(2 marks)*

Study tip   Only 2 marks are available so you do not have to give a detailed explanation.

(b)   Explain Muslim beliefs about the purpose of life.   *(4 marks)*

Study tip   To gain full marks here you need to show a clear knowledge and understanding of Muslim teachings on this concept. It may be helpful to include examples in your answer to clarify the points you make.

(c)   'A Muslim must always be prepared to fight in a war.'
Do you agree? Give reasons for your answer, showing that you have thought about more than one point of view. Refer to Muslim teaching in your answer.   *(6 marks)*

Study tip   You can agree, disagree or be undecided about these statements. Remember that you must give reasons for at least two points of view and conclude with your supported opinion.

(d)   Explain differing Muslim attitudes to nuclear disarmament.   *(6 marks)*

Study tip   Here you will need to show that Muslims can have differing views on whether or not it is acceptable for countries to have nuclear weapons.

(e)   'Protests are a waste of time, they cannot change anything.'
Do you agree? Give reasons for your answer, showing that you have thought about more than one point of view. Refer to Muslim teachings in your answer.   *(6 marks)*

Study tip   In these longer evaluation questions it is worth spending a few moments planning out how you are going to structure your response. Remember to include more than one point of view.

4 The environment

4.1 The created world

Muslim beliefs about creation

Muslims believe that Islam began with the creation of man by Allah. People were created to serve God and obey his will. This teaching can be found in the Muslim creation story recorded in the *Qur'an*. The story makes clear that there is one God, Allah, and that God is great and his creation was perfect and good. Allah created an order in the world and made human beings khalifahs (stewards) of his creation. This means that human beings have the responsibility to care for and look after creation. Allah created

A   The Qur'an teaches the world was created by Allah

all life and Muslims believe they should be thankful for this gift. The earth and everything on it belongs to God and is entrusted to mankind until the Day of Judgement.

Allah chose to make humans superior to everything else in creation. He also ordained that they would have the opportunity through their lives on earth to earn an eternal life in paradise. Allah gave people free will. This means that they have the freedom to choose their own path in life. Allah also ordained a way of life for people to follow. However, people must freely choose to submit to Allah's will. If they do this, then life on Earth will be good. The term Islam means 'submission and peace' and Muslims believe that they have a personal jihad, to live their lives devoted to striving in the path of Allah.

Objectives

Understand why Muslims value the created world.

Key terms

Khalifa(h): stewardship. The belief that believers have a duty to look after the environment on behalf of God.

links

Read pages 78–79 and pages 94–95 for more on stewardship.

B   Allah provided mankind with all they needed

'Allah created the world and it belongs to him.'

'The earth provides us with everything we need.'

'The beauty of the natural world brings me closer to Allah.'

'I can serve Allah by acting as his khalifah.'

C   Why Muslims value the created world

links

The term 'jihad' is defined on page 58.

Muslim teaching about creation

The *Qur'an* does not have a creation story as such, but there are many references to aspects of creation. The key points are summarised in the story below.

Before time existed there was only Allah. Allah created the universe with his divine word 'Be'. He made the heavens, the world and everything that lives upon it. He created the angels, the sun, the moon and the stars and placed them in an ordered universe. He made the world rich with creatures that could swim, crawl, walk and fly and caused the earth to bring forth all vegetation.

Allah commanded his angels to bring him seven handfuls of different coloured sand from the earth. Allah moulded the sand into a form of a man and breathed life into him. He called the man Adam and placed him in paradise. Seeing that Adam needed a partner he created Eve from Adam's side. Allah then taught Adam the names of all the animals and commanded the angels to bow to Adam. However, the angel Iblis would not do this and refused to obey Allah's will.

Adam and Eve lived in a beautiful garden, paradise. But one day the evil Iblis tempted them to eat the fruit from the only tree that Allah had forbidden to them. Allah knew that Adam and Eve had disobeyed him and so threw them out of paradise and sent them to live on the earth. However, because Allah is merciful, the earth Allah had created provided them with all they needed. Allah also decreed that if human beings submit to his will they will be saved and taken to live an eternal life in paradise.

Extension activity

How is the creation of people different to the creation of all other forms of life? What can Muslims learn from this story about their relationship with God, with other people and with the natural world?

D   *Adam and Eve lived in a beautiful garden, paradise*

Beliefs and teachings

O mankind! We created you from a single male and female and made you into nations and tribes.

Qur'an 49:13

He it is who created the heavens and the earth in six days – and His Throne was over the waters.

Qur'an 11:7

And the firmament has he raised high, and He has set up the Balance (of justice).

Qur'an 55:7

Study tip

When discussing why Muslims value the created world, refer to beliefs, teachings and practical reasons.

Activities

1. Make a list of key points the *Qur'an* teaches about creation.
2. Explain what this story teaches Muslims about God.
3. Explain why Muslims value the created world.
4. 'People will always put themselves before everything else in creation.' What do you think? Explain your opinion.

Research activity

Find some examples from the *Hadith* that show the importance of the natural world. Use these to make a leaflet that explains why Muslims value the created world.

Summary

You should now know why Muslims value the created world.

4.2 Stewardship

Stewardship

The concept of stewardship underpins all Islamic teaching about creation. It is the basis of Muslim responses to all issues concerning the environment. Allah created the earth and entrusted people with the role of khalifah. This means that Muslims have a responsibility to care for the earth and strive to maintain the harmony and balance that Allah created. They are also accountable to Allah on the Day of Judgement for how well they have fulfilled this role.

Beliefs and teachings

Allah has made you His custodians of the Earth.

Qur'an 6:165

The creation of the heavens and the Earth is more awesome than the creation of human beings, but most people do not know this.

Qur'an 40:57

The principles of stewardship

The central belief in tawhid (the oneness of God) is at the heart of all Islamic ethics. There is one God, Allah, and everything comes to be because he wills it. It therefore follows that people are part of a harmonious creation, enjoying a special relationship with their creator and everything else in the environment. Allah has placed knowledge and wisdom in people, which is part of their human nature; Muslims call this fitra. The world was created in such a way that it works in harmony and balance; Muslims call this mizan. It is human actions based on selfish greed that has led to many of the environmental problems that the world faces today. As khalifahs or stewards, Muslims have a responsibility to do what they can to bring about change and restore the earth for Allah.

A *The Earth was created in perfect balance and harmony*

Tawhid (Unity)	Fitra (Nature)	Mizan (Balance)	Khalifah (Responsibility)

The Practice of Stewardship

Individuals	Community	National	International
All Muslims have a responsibility to do what they can to care for the environment. Avoiding waste, buying eco-friendly products and recycling are all ways they can help.	Community leaders and members can encourage and spread the need for stewardship of the earth and its resources. Sermons, teaching and collaborative projects can all help to make a difference.	Leaders of Islamic nations have to act to preserve and protect the areas they govern. By establishing just laws, making conservation zones and regulating industry they can steward the environment responsibly.	Islam requires leaders to work with others, regardless of faith, to bring about justice and harmony in the world. Islamic nations participate fully in earth summits and other aspects of the UN to represent the views of the Islamic world on the need to steward the earth's resources now and for the future.

B *Muslim environmental ethics*

C   *On Judgement Day the sparrow will cry out, 'Why did you kill me for no good purpose?'*

Case study

The Prophet King Solomon

The *Qur'an* records that King Solomon had been given the gift of being able to understand the birds and the animals. In *Qur'an* 27:16 Solomon says that 'We have been taught the speech of birds, and on us has been bestowed all things, this is indeed Grace manifest from Allah.' One day when he was marching with his army he came upon a valley of ants. The story tells how he was able to understand the ants' panic and reflect on the marvel of creation. Other stories recount how animals aided Solomon in his rule and how his gift enabled him to act with wisdom and compassion.

This story illustrates that when a Muslim is in harmony with his creator and his environment he will receive gifts and grace from Allah. Solomon's wisdom and greatness as a ruler were achieved because he was able to show compassion for all of creation, even the tiny ant.

D   *Even the smallest creature has a part in the world*

Discussion activity

In small groups, discuss how having faith might encourage a believer to participate in activities that help to preserve the natural environment.

Activities

1   Explain why stewardship is important to Muslims.

2   a   Explain the terms tawhid, fitra, mizan and khalifah.

    b   Why are they important in stewardship?

3   Describe some of the ways that Muslims have contributed to stewardship of the world.

4   What does the story of Solomon teach Muslims about their relationship with the natural world?

5   'Environmental problems will only be solved if everyone works together.' What do you think? Give reasons for your answer showing that you have thought about more than one point of view. Refer to Islam in your answer.

Extension activity

Working with a partner, find a poem about the beauty of the natural world. Make a PowerPoint presentation to illustrate the poem and then share this with the rest of your class.

Summary

You should now know and understand Muslim teaching about and attitudes to stewardship.

Study tip

Using technical terms such as stewardship helps to show your understanding of a topic.

4.3 Causes of pollution (1)

What is pollution?

Pollution describes anything that contaminates the soil, water, landscape or atmosphere with harmful or unsightly consequences. Pollution occurs mainly because of human activity. The use of natural resources for energy, the production methods in some industries and the by-products of our lifestyles have had a seriously damaging effect on our environment. This is a concern because pollution is a global problem and its impact affects all living things on the planet.

Types of pollution

There are many different types of pollution that can be broadly grouped into the following headings:

- Air pollution – occurs when harmful chemicals and gases are released into the air we breathe. This is one of the most damaging types of pollution, because pollutants in the air can be carried thousands of miles. For example, in April 1986 a nuclear reactor at a power plant in Chernobyl, Ukraine exploded. The radioactive cloud from the disaster spread over many European countries affecting many people, farm animals and forests.

- Water pollution – occurs when harmful liquid waste products are released into oceans, lakes and rivers. These have an immediate damaging effect on the water environment and spread into the soil through the water cycle. For example, the build-up of algae which reduces the oxygen levels kills other organisms such as fish and coral.

- Land/soil pollution – occurs when toxic waste is buried in the ground causing chemical changes in the composition of the soil. This makes the land infertile. It also occurs with the accumulation of non-biodegradable waste. Modern manufacturing produces large quantities of materials that do not easily rot away into the soil. These products are dumped in landfill sites making areas unsightly and the land unusable.

Causes of pollution

Natural disasters such as volcanic eruptions can cause pollution, but most of it is caused by human activity. Industry creates all kinds of pollution through the manufacturing process. Every day, transportation by cars, buses, lorries and planes emits CO_2 (carbon dioxide) gas and other fumes into the atmosphere. Lifestyles in the western world consume vast quantities of resources that produce tonnes and tonnes of rubbish. Our energy needs require the burning of fossil fuels which releases CO_2 into the atmosphere and this in turn has contributed to the greenhouse effect. Millions of litres of liquid waste and sewage are poured into rivers and seas. The simple fact is that unless more effort is put into conservation and environmentally sound technologies, the earth is in danger of becoming uninhabitable!

Objectives

Understand the main causes of pollution.

Key terms

Pollution: the act of harming or contaminating the environment.

A Smoke pollution is a by-product of oil refineries

Discussion activity

In a small group, discuss what you think are the main effects of pollution on people and wildlife. Can you think of any other types of pollution? Share your ideas with the rest of the class.

B Modern lifestyles create huge quantities of waste

Islamic attitudes to pollution

Islam teaches that all Muslims should behave correctly and act in a way that respects all living things. It is important to care for and protect the environment because it benefits everyone. The teachings of the *Qur'an* make clear that Allah has given people the responsibility of caring for the earth. This means that Muslims should do all they can to maintain Allah's creation. Irresponsible behaviour that leads to pollution is wrong. Muslims understand that God has given human beings the responsibility of stewardship, a duty to care for the environment. The *Qur'an* gives guidance for Muslims in the conduct of business. It stresses that there must be justice and fairness. These principles should also be applied to the environment because the harmful effects of pollution affect everyone.

> **C**   *Convenience – but at what price to the environment? Disposable nappies are the third most common item in landfill sites in Europe, America, Japan and Australia. They take over 200 years to decompose*

Beliefs and teachings

Mischief has appeared on land and sea because of (the meed) that the hands of men have earned, that Allah may give them a taste of some of their deeds: In order that they may turn back (from Evil).

Qur'an 30:41

Activities

1. Describe the main types of pollution.
2. Explain **three** effects of pollution on people and the natural world.
3. Explain Muslim attitudes to pollution.
4. 'A Muslim should not work for a company that is polluting the environment.' What do you think? Explain your answer.

Study tip

Your answers will have depth if you write about different types of pollution.

Ecotourism in Zanzibar

Case study

Chumbe is an island just 8 miles off the beautiful coastline of Zanzibar. It is a model for how an industry can be developed without causing pollution and destroying the natural landscape. The Islamic government of Zanzibar introduced laws banning fishing and other activities to preserve the delicate coral reefs. Whilst this was good for the environment it presented problems for the local people who were dependent on the fishing industry. Through the development of ecotourism new jobs were created providing services to the growing number of tourists coming to the area. The island has now become an official marine sanctuary and its growing popularity as a destination for snorkelling and diving has secured a prosperous future for the local people.

Research activity

Find out more about ecotourism and how it protects the interests of the environment and the people who live there.

Extension activity

Find out more about environmental issues at:
www.keepbanderabeautiful.org

Summary

You should now know about the causes of pollution and understand Muslim attitudes to pollution.

4.4 Causes of pollution (2)

■ Pollution – global impact

The consequences of pollution have had a global impact. The environment and atmosphere of the planet have suffered major harm because of the activities of mankind. This affects everyone and everything living on the earth. This has raised important ethical questions about the way we use the earth's natural resources and our responsibilities now and to future generations.

Global warming

The greenhouse effect is the natural process by which the sun's energy is trapped in the earth's atmosphere by a blanket of gases. This keeps the planet warm enough to sustain life. However, the burning of fossil fuels over many decades has added to this blanket of gases. As a result, there has been a gradual increase in the temperature of the planet. In addition to this, the destruction of the ozone layer which prevents harmful rays entering the earth's atmosphere is also adding to the problem of global warming. This is resulting in the melting of the ice caps and rising sea levels. Changes in temperatures and the effects of pollution are having devastating effects on some of the earth's most fragile ecosystems such as Antarctica.

When it's cold and rainy, it's easy to joke in the UK that a bit of a warmer climate would be a good thing. However, climate change is having damaging effects around the globe. Rising sea levels have resulted in increased flooding in low-lying areas and the loss of valuable farming land for vulnerable communities in poor areas such as Bangladesh. In other areas, increased temperatures and reduced rainfall is contributing to droughts and the growth of desert areas in countries such as Ghana and Nigeria. This leads to famine and nomadic communities being forced to give up their culture and lifestyle. There are also the environmental losses as wildlife loses further habitat. Eventually wildlife will be in danger of extinction (see Table **A** of endangered species).

> **Objectives**
>
> Understand the global consequences of pollution.

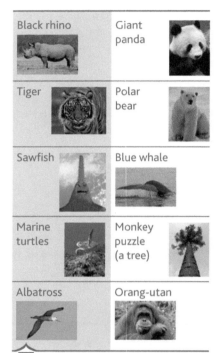

Black rhino	Giant panda
Tiger	Polar bear
Sawfish	Blue whale
Marine turtles	Monkey puzzle (a tree)
Albatross	Orang-utan

A Habitat loss caused by global warming, pollution and overuse of the resources has left many species on the brink of extinction

Deforestation

Rainforests cover approximately 10 per cent of the earth's land surface and are an essential part of regulating the earth's climate. Trees and plant life use carbon dioxide and emit oxygen, which is essential for all animal life. Every year large areas of rainforest are cleared to make way for grazing land or to provide land for industry and building. The burning of the forests also contributes to carbon dioxide pollution in the atmosphere. This is brought about because of the pressures of the global economy. The rainforests lie predominantly in less developed nations. They are forced to use this natural resource in order to compete with other economies in the world. The destruction of the rainforests is contributing to the effects of global warming as more carbon dioxide remains in the air.

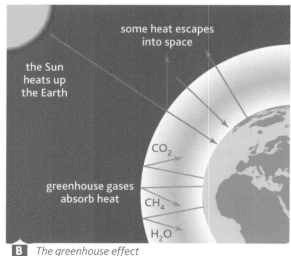

some heat escapes into space

the Sun heats up the Earth

CO_2

greenhouse gases absorb heat

CH_4

H_2O

B The greenhouse effect

This is having a major impact on the environment. It is estimated that 50 per cent of the earth's flora and fauna are found in the rainforests. Most medicines are created from natural plant sources. The loss of habitat is leading to the extinction of species that may have held the cure to cancer or AIDS for example. We simply do not know; if the species has been wiped out no research can be undertaken. The increase in harmful gases in the air may also be responsible for a number of illnesses caused by breathing in harmful gases such as cancers and respiratory disorders. Native peoples are losing their traditional way of life and are often forced into living in poverty. Wildlife is also endangered; as their habitats are reduced, so too are their populations. There are now more species of mammals than ever, in danger of extinction.

Sustainability

The rate at which natural resources are consumed is leading to a crisis of long-term sustainability. Fossil fuels, minerals, ores and rainforests take hundreds, thousands or even millions of years to form. Once these resources are used up they are gone forever. We are now using these non-renewable resources at a greater rate than ever before. The excessive use is also contributing to the effects of pollution and raises questions about the impact this will have on future generations. The need to provide for present generations must be balanced against the needs of people in the future. Unless action is taken now to conserve and protect natural resources, there will be long-term problems in the future.

C *The rainforests are home to 50 per cent of the world's species of animals and plants*

D *Indigenous tribes are losing their livelihoods because of the pressures of global economics*

Muslim attitudes to the environment

Muslims believe that the environment and all that is in it belongs to Allah. People have a responsibility to care for creation and to use Allah's gifts wisely. The world was created in harmony and balance. Allah put in place a perfect natural order that provided for the needs of all in his creation. The exploitation of the earth's natural resources and the consequences of this are very wrong. Human activity driven by greed, selfishness and injustice has brought about the environmental crisis that faces the world today. Muslims believe they have a duty and responsibility to Allah to do all they can to address the problems that have been created, for Allah and for future generations.

Summary

You should now know about the causes and consequences of pollution and Muslim attitudes to this.

Research activity

Find out more about endangered species at www.endangeredspecie.com and www.worldwide.org/species

links

Look up the meaning of the terms 'sustainability' and 'extinction' in the Glossary at the back of this book.

Activities

1 Describe the effects of global warming.
2 Explain **three** effects of the loss of rainforests.
3 Explain why pollution has an impact on the climate.
4 What is sustainability? Why is it important?
5 'There are more important issues for Muslims than caring for the environment.' What do you think? Explain your opinion.

Extension activity

Design a poster to be displayed in a Mosque school to encourage children to care for the environment. Include ideas for how they can do this and why they have this responsibility as Muslims.

Study tip

Being able to refer in your answers to the principal values of Islam such as justice will show good understanding.

4.5 Conservation

What is conservation?

It is clear that the consequences of pollution and other environmental problems will not resolve themselves. It is for this reason that conservation has become an important environmental issue and a global concern. If the planet is going to be able to continue to sustain life on earth, both the causes and the devastating effects of pollution need to be addressed.

The conservation movement seeks to address the many environmental issues. It is concerned with protecting natural fragile environments such as the rainforests. It is involved with projects to preserve and protect animals and other species in danger of extinction because of the loss of habitats. Conservation also involves finding ways to manage industries that rely on non-renewable resources such as fossil fuels. This also extends to those industries which are in danger of over exploiting stocks such as fishing and timber. The aim is to find a balance between present needs and those of future generations.

A *Alternative energy sources can help to conserve fossil fuels*

B *Hydro-electric power station*

Muslim teaching about conservation

The *Qur'an* gives Muslims clear principles that can be applied to the issue of conservation. Tawhid is the clear teaching of the oneness of Allah. Everything in creation exists because God willed it to be. The unity of all creation and the natural order which is in place is because Allah made it that way. Muslims believe they must submit fully to Allah's will and He will provide for their physical, emotional and spiritual needs. The universe and all within it belongs to God and all living beings respond to God in praise and worship. It therefore follows that caring for creation is essential in showing submission to the will of Allah, the creator of all things.

C *Some people have put solar panels on their roofs to help reduce their carbon footprint*

Beliefs and teachings

To Him belong all the things in the heavens and on earth.

Qur'an 4:171

To Him belongs every being that is in the heavens and on earth: all are devoutly obedient to Him.

Qur'an 30:26

Allah's care for His creatures is universal.

Qur'an 62:1

links

The term 'khalifah' is defined on page 76.

Allah placed people above everything else in creation. The *Qur'an* teaches that Allah gave human beings a sacred duty as khalifahs, guardians over all creation. He placed in people the knowledge and wisdom to carry out this duty, but he also gave them the free will to make decisions for themselves. Only human beings have this ability to reason and to act with justice and compassion. The *Qur'an* teaches Muslims that the earth is a gift from Allah to be used for good to meet their needs. However, it also warns against extravagance and being wasteful. The power given to people by God should be limited by the responsibilities they have to God, other people and all of creation. Allah has entrusted people with the duty to maintain the balance in nature that he has created.

D   *Habitat loss and hunting have made the tiger an endangered species*

Beliefs and teachings

Eat and drink but waste not by excess for Allah loves not the wasters.

Qur'an 7:31

Activities

1   Explain the term conservation.
2   Explain **two** reasons why conservation is important.
3   Describe **two** examples of conservation.
4   Explain Muslim teaching about conservation.
5   'The earth is ours; we can do what we want with it.' Do you agree? Give reasons for your answer, showing that you have thought about more than one point of view. Refer to Islam in your answer.

Research activity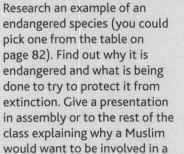

Research an example of an endangered species (you could pick one from the table on page 82). Find out why it is endangered and what is being done to try to protect it from extinction. Give a presentation in assembly or to the rest of the class explaining why a Muslim would want to be involved in a project to protect the animal.

Summary

You should now know and understand why Muslims believe conservation is important.

Study tip

Being able to give examples will help to develop your responses.

4.6 Muslim responses to conservation

How does Islam respond to conservation?

Individual responses

As a khalifah for Allah, each Muslim can do something to help to conserve the environment. In the modern world there is now a lot of information on how individuals can help with the global issues related to pollution. Many Muslims play their part in helping, by trying to be eco-friendly. The *Qur'an* encourages Muslims not to be wasteful, to use what they need and not to be overly extravagant. These are some of the ways they do this:

- **Recycle** things like glass, paper and cans.
- Buy products with less packaging.
- Choose products that are recycled or from sustainable sources.
- Avoid waste by using what is needed and limiting excess.
- Cut fuel consumption in the home and when travelling.
- Reuse things like carrier bags.
- Make compost.
- Give to charity shops rather than throwing things away.
- Support environmental initiatives locally and globally.

Beliefs and teachings

Eat of the good things we have provided for you, but commit no excess.

Qur'an 20:81

Community responses

Islam teaches that conservation is a responsibility for all Muslims and recognises that, in order to do this, it is necessary to work with others. In 1986, leaders from the Islamic community joined with members of all faiths at a special conference held in Assisi. Its aim was to produce a faith response to environmental issues. This has become known as the Assisi Declarations and includes teachings from all of the world's major faith traditions.

The Islamic view reflects the belief in tawhid and the unity of all creation put in place by Allah. The responsibility of caring for the earth was entrusted to people as Allah's khalifahs. On the Day of Judgement all will be accountable for their actions on earth. Islam does not have a specific harvest festival which celebrates the importance of the earth. However, Muslims regularly give thanks to Allah in their daily prayers for the goodness of the earth and God's gifts to them.

For Muslim communities it is important to participate in local, regional and national initiatives that are directed at caring for the earth. For example, in the London borough of Tower Hamlets, where 45 per cent of the population is Muslim, a joint project with the council and the mosques led to an increase in recycling. Friday sermons, coffee mornings, an exhibition and leaflets in several languages, relating the teaching of the *Qur'an* on conservation, were used successfully to bring about change.

Objectives

Understand Muslim responses to conservation:
- as individuals
- as a community
- as international partners.

Key terms

Recycling: (the act of) reusing substances to save waste or help the environment.

Earth Summit: a world conference about the environment.

Discussion activity

In a small group, discuss the suggestions for being eco-friendly. What are their advantages and disadvantages? Can you think of any other ways to be eco-friendly? Share your group's ideas with the rest of the class.

A *There are many ways to recycle*

∞ links

Look up the word 'tawhid' in the Glossary at the back of this book.

Recycle things like glass, paper and cans	Buy products with less packaging	Cut fuel consumption in the home and travelling
Choose products that are recycled or from sustainable sources		Avoid waste by using what is needed and limiting excess
Reuse things like carrier bags, make compost etc	Support environmental iniatives locally and globally	Give to charity shops rather than throw away

B *Leaflets were one way that Tower Hamlets and the Muslim community increased recycling in the community*

Earth Summits

The need for global action on environmental issues was first highlighted by the Brundtland Report 'Our Common Future' in 1987. It introduced the idea of 'sustainable development' which it explained as meeting the needs of present generations without compromising the ability of future generations to meet their needs. This has led to a number of **Earth Summits** at which Islamic nations have participated in developing policies and guidelines for all nations to follow. The aims of the UN Economic and Social Development Agency to eliminate poverty and establish sustainable development are in keeping with the principles of justice and stewardship in Islam.

Islamic nations have also worked together to produce collaborative responses to environmental issues. The first Islamic conference for ministers of the environment took place in Jeddah, Saudi Arabia, in 2002. The meeting produced a number of frameworks for environmental protection and sustainable development reflecting the views of the Islamic world.

Research activity

Find out more about the UN and environmental issues at **www.un.org/esa**

Beliefs and teachings

The Earth is green and beautiful and Allah has made you His stewards over it.

Hadith

Activities

1 Describe **three** ways that Muslims can contribute personally to conservation.

2 What are the Assisi Declarations?

3 How can Muslim communities help with green initiatives?

4 Explain how Islamic countries have participated in working towards a sustainable future.

5 'Caring for the earth is the most important duty a Muslim has.' How far do you agree? Give reasons for your answer showing that you have thought about more than one point of view.

Extension activity

Imagine you have been invited to speak at the opening of the next Earth Summit. Write a speech that you would give to convince those present that they should do more to protect the environment. Remember that you will be representing young people around the world and your address is being given to the world's leaders.

Study tip

You could be asked specifically about individual, community, national or international responses to conservation.

Summary

You should now know and understand Muslim individual, community and global responses to conservation.

4.7 Muslim conservation case study

The Islamic Foundation for Ecology and Environmental Sciences

Based in Birmingham, the Islamic Foundation for Ecology and Environmental Sciences (IFEES) is one of the leading Islamic environmental organisations. It aims to increase awareness of Muslim teaching about conservation, change attitudes and behaviour that have led to environmental problems, and to alleviate the poverty these problems cause. The organisation takes a lead in many areas including practical conservation projects, providing training, and working internationally with governments, Muslim environmental activists and others to bring about change. Their publication EcoIslam covers a range of environmental issues in the news and provides information on the work and progress of IFEES projects around the globe.

Objectives

Understand how Muslims are contributing to international conservation projects.

A *Logo of IFEES*

Case study

IFEES conservation projects – Indonesia

The tsunami on 26 December 2004 was one of the worst natural disasters the world has ever seen. When the tsunami had gone, it was clear that Aceh, a province of Indonesia, was one of the most devastated areas. Thousands had been killed and the landscape had vanished. Since then a great deal of work has been done to help people rebuild their homes and lives. The projects there have also looked to address the environmental issues. In rebuilding, they have tried to find ways to conserve and protect the landscape and fishing for the years and the generations to come.

IFEES has adopted the village of Gunung Mas in Indonesia and has helped to develop eco-friendly energy using the river as a source. They have established traditional farming methods and reforested the landscape to create a working eco-village. This is not only good for conservation, but also helps to protect the lifestyle and culture of the people who live there. They are also working to conserve the Indonesian rainforest which is a world heritage site.

B *The 2004 tsunami devastated Aceh in Indonesia*

Zanzibar

Mizali is an uninhabited island in the Pacific Ocean. It is a designated marine conservation area and its coastline is rich with coral, tropical fish and turtle nesting grounds. However, its survival was threatened. The local Muslim fishermen were using dynamite to increase their catches because international trawlers had depleted the fish stocks. These practices were destroying the fragile ecosystem and would have led to the collapse of the fishermen's community. Through a programme of teaching and training, IFEES has been able to work with the Mizali fishermen to help them change their methods. It was able to help the fishermen understand their responsibilities as khalifahs and this brought about the change that government laws had failed to achieve. IFEES is campaigning to have Mizali declared a hima which is a Shari'ah-based conservation zone. This means that the area will be conserved using Islamic laws. It is hoped that by doing this the mostly Muslim population will continue to adhere to the conservation efforts made in the area.

C *Coral reefs are amongst the most fragile marine environments*

Case study

Activities

1 What are the aims of IFEES?

2 How does the conservation project in Aceh reflect Muslim teachings about conservation?

3 The Mizali fishermen refused to comply with the laws forbidding them to use dynamite. Why do you think IFEES was able to bring about changes that laws could not?

4 'Conservation will only work if there is justice.' What do you think? Explain your opinion.

Research activity 🔍

Find out more about IFEES and Muslim conservation work at:
www.ifees.org.uk

Summary

You should now know and understand the work IFEES is doing to contribute to international conservation efforts.

Extension activity

Design a poster to advertise the work of the IFEES.

Discussion activity 👥

Organisations like the IFEES should be funded by the government. Prepare arguments for and against this statement and hold a class debate.

Study tip

If you are asked about conservation, describing specific examples of Muslim-led conservation projects will show depth of understanding. You can use IFEES or any other example you have studied.

4.8 Animal rights

Should animals have rights?

We share the planet with many thousands of different species of animal and they play an important part in life on earth. People use animals in many ways: for work, companionship, clothing and food to name just a few. Some activities involve working with animals. However, others use animals to meet human needs or desires. Many people would consider human life to be more important than animal life. But does this give us the right to use animals in any way we choose?

When we look at the animal kingdom we can see that human beings and animals have some things in common. Animals share the basic characteristics of life such as the need to eat, breathe and reproduce. Animals are able to sense or feel things; they share companionship and express emotions and feelings. For example, a dog wags its tail when happy and excited but holds it down when upset or afraid. Animals are able to communicate and some live in social groups, demonstrating behaviour similar to human families. Animals are also clearly able to suffer and feel pain. Given that animals have this in common with humans, should they also have rights?

A An animal rights protest

B Animals are able to express feelings

What are animal rights?

The term 'rights' is linked to ideas of justice and fairness. It means to have legal or moral protection. Whether or not animals should have rights is an ethical question. There is a wide range of views on this issue. Some people are animal liberationists who feel that animals should be treated equally. Such people are prepared to go to extreme lengths to campaign for what they believe in. For example, they may attack organisations and individuals who use animals for research or participate in hunting. At the other end of the scale there are people who feel animals are there to be used in any way humans choose.

Muslim attitudes to animal rights

Islam recognises the value of animals as part of the created world. Animals are a gift from Allah for humans to use but not to abuse. Human life is more important because Allah has made it that way. Unlike animals, humans have the ability to reason and act upon intelligence with justice and compassion. The behaviour of animals is instinctive and follows the natural laws put in place by God. Animals do have a right to be treated with respect, but humans have Allah's permission to use them to meet human needs.

Discussion activity

2 Discuss the views expressed on animal rights. How far do you agree with their attitudes? Share your views in a class discussion.

> I am a vegetarian. I do not eat animals because it is wrong to kill, and all life is valuable. I believe animals should be treated with respect. I would like to see a world where people work with animals sharing the planet and not causing unnecessary suffering. There is nothing wrong with having pets and using animals for work, but they must be properly cared for.

> Animals are there for us to use. They aren't the same as people and I don't think it matters how we use them. They are a resource just like everything else on the planet. I think there are more important issues to address than animal rights. What's the point in making laws to ban hunting when there are thousands of homeless people on the streets?

> I am an animal rights activist. Animals cannot speak for themselves so they need people like me to stand up for them. I see nothing wrong with disrupting businesses which make money out of the suffering of innocent animals. I am prepared to go to prison if I have to. Someone has to make a stand against animal abuse.

> I think animals should have some rights. In this day and age, animals shouldn't be being abused just for entertainment. Wild animals need protection; otherwise some species are going to become extinct. I don't think it's wrong to use animals for human needs as we are the superior species, but I don't think there should be unnecessary cruelty.

C *Some views on animal rights*

Extension activity

2 Look at this website for more on Muslim teaching on all aspects of animal rights: www.themodernreligion.com

Activities

1 How are animals like humans?
2 In what ways are animals different to humans?
3 What does the term 'animal rights' mean?
4 What does Islam teach about animal rights?
5 'People are more important than animals.' How far do you agree? Give reasons for your answer showing that you have thought about more than one point of view.

Research activity

Find out about some of the occasions when the Prophet Muhammad spoke about or encountered animals. Write a summary of these in a leaflet explaining Muslim teaching about animal rights.

Summary

You should now know and understand the meaning of animal rights and Muslim attitudes to animals.

Study tip

When explaining a technical term, such as animal rights, using examples can help to make clear what you mean.

What does Islam teach about animals?

Islam teaches that animals are important in creation. Human beings have been given dominion or power over them, but this does not mean that they can be abused. All of creation is aware of God and animals worship God in their own way. Muslims believe that animals are a gift from Allah which is to be used, but this must be for good reasons. This means that Muslims would not agree with any cruel use of animals that is entirely for human pleasure not needs. The Prophet strictly forbade blood sports and once chastised a man who sharpened a knife in front of the animal he was about to slaughter.

> ### Beliefs and teachings
>
> The heavens, the earth and all beings ... declare His glory.
>
> *Qur'an* 17:44
>
> Lawful unto you for food, are all four footed animals with the exceptions named.
>
> *Qur'an* 5:1
>
> If someone kills a sparrow for sport it will cry out on the Day of Judgement, 'They killed me for no good purpose.'
>
> *Hadith*

Throughout the *Qur'an* and the *Hadith* there are many references giving guidance on the treatment of animals. Animals should not be caged and removed from their natural environment. Muslims would not approve of zoos, circuses or of having non-domesticated animals as pets. However, it is permitted to cage an animal if it is suffering and needs help. Muslims would accept that zoos and safari parks that are taking part in preserving and protecting wildlife could be supported. Most modern zoos, especially those in Britain, are involved in conservation projects.

Objectives

Understand Muslim attitudes to caring for animals.

A *Muslims believe animals should not be kept in cages*

B *Nature reserves protect animals from extinction*

Muslim views on farming animals

Islam permits the use of animals for food, vegetarianism not being widely practised amongst Muslims. Muslims are allowed to domesticate and farm animals for the purpose of food, but they should be treated with respect and cared for. Modern intensive farming practices such as battery hens and veal cages are strictly against the principles of justice and compassion in Islam. Farming animals in such a way is considered cruel and unnecessary. Muslims should use traditional or organic farming methods.

Food that is permitted in Islam is called halal and that which is forbidden is called haram. For meat to be halal it must have been farmed and slaughtered according to Muslim teaching. This is laid out in the Shari'ah law and Muslims are forbidden to eat meat not prepared in this way. Islam also teaches that certain animals such as pigs and any animal that has not been ritually slaughtered according to halal rules are forbidden as food.

C   *Farm animals should be treated with respect and well cared for*

The rules state that animals to be slaughtered must be healthy and well cared for. When the animal is brought for slaughter, it must have its throat cut quickly by a single action to reduce the pain inflicted. As this is done the shahadah is recited and then all blood must drain from the carcass. Also animals must not be slaughtered in front of other animals. Some Islamic ceremonies include the ritual slaughter of animals for food as part of the celebrations. This meat is distributed to support the poor.

D   *Factory farming is strictly forbidden in Islam*

Extension activity

Using the internet or a library, find out about Eid ul Adha and Islamic birth ceremonies. Write a report that explains why animals are slaughtered on these occasions and what responsibilities Muslims have to these animals.

Activities

1. Explain Islamic teaching about the care of animals.
2. Explain Muslim attitudes to farming animals.
3. Choose **three** other uses of animals and explain Muslim attitudes to them.

Summary

You should now know and understand Muslim attitudes to the care and treatment of animals.

Study tip

Remember, your opinion on an issue must include reasons not just personal thoughts.

4.10 Animal experimentation

Using animals for experimentation in research

Objectives

Understand Islamic attitudes to animal experimentation.

There is widespread use of live animals for many different kinds of experimentation in research. Every year millions of animals are used to conduct experiments to further human knowledge and understanding of the world in which we live. Most animals used in research are bred specifically for that purpose. Also, experiments involving higher order mammals make up a very small percentage of the total animals used. In some countries there are strict regulations about the use of animals in research. However, some people feel that this is not enough and that all animal experimentation should be stopped.

A *Reasons for and against experiments using animals*

Reasons for:	Reasons against:
Medicine would not advance without these experiments.	New technology means experiments can be done without animals.
Animals used are mostly rodents bred for the purpose.	Many experiments are unnecessary repetitions.
Human lives are saved by this research.	Animals are experimented on to develop luxuries like cosmetics.
Most experiments are conducted with anaesthetic; animal suffering is minimal.	Animals react differently to humans; tests are unreliable.
Many drugs would not have been developed without this research.	Causing deliberate suffering is cruel and inhumane.
Animals also benefit because the research contributes to veterinary practices.	All animals, however small, should be treated with respect.

Discussion activity

'There is nothing wrong with testing new medicines and surgical procedures on animals.' Prepare arguments for and against this statement and then hold a class debate. Take a vote at the end based on the quality of the arguments presented.

B *Penicillin is fatal to guinea pigs*

Research activity

Find out about the protests made by one animal liberation organisation. Write a newspaper report about their activities.

Muslim attitudes to animal experimentation

Islam does not forbid animal experimentation if it is for a good purpose. Animals can be used to help further human understanding. Where the research is for the development of medicine, Islam would accept this since a greater good would be achieved. However, the animals used must be treated humanely and well cared for. Experiments conducted must be for good purposes such as the development of drugs and surgical techniques. If the research is to meet genuine human needs, then it is allowed. Where experiments are necessary, the animals must have their suffering minimised. The tests should not be unnecessarily repeated and, where alternatives to animal research are available, they should be used. Students are not allowed to conduct experiments on live animals.

Islam considers experimenting on animals for luxuries such as cosmetics is wrong. It also forbids experiments such as those to find out the effects of smoking, because this is self-inflicted human suffering. Killing animals to satisfy human vanity and desires is against the principles of Islam and conflicts with the teaching of stewardship. Allah provided animals to help people, not to satisfy selfish whims. Whilst there are no specific teachings on animal experimentation in the *Qur'an*, the principles of justice, kindness and compassion should always be applied.

C   *Alternative research to animal experimentation should be used*

D   *Experimenting on animals for luxuries such as make up is considered wrong*

Beliefs and teachings

Whoever kills anything bigger than a sparrow without just cause will be accountable to Allah.

Hadith

Activities

1   What is animal experimentation?
2   Why is experimentation on animals carried out?
3   Explain **three** reasons why some people think animal experimentation is wrong.
4   Explain Muslim attitudes to using animals for experimentation in research.
5   'Muslims should never buy a product tested on animals.' What do you think? Explain your opinion.

Study tip

When writing about controversial issues, make sure that you can argue reasons on both sides of the issue.

Summary

You should now know and understand Muslim attitudes to experimenting on animals.

Assessment guidance

4

The environment – summary

For the examination you should now be able to:

✔ show a knowledge of Muslim views of stewardship and the value of the natural world, and explain how these beliefs influence Muslim attitudes to:

 – the created world

 – the causes of pollution

 – conservation

 – individual, community, national and international responses to conservation, including recycling, conservation projects and Earth Summits

 – animal rights

 – care of animals

 – use of animals for experimentation in research

 – stewardship.

Sample answer

1 Write an answer to the following question:

Explain Muslim attitudes to conservation. Use examples in your answer. *(6 marks)*

2 Read the following sample answer:

> Muslims think that conservation is a good thing. They are told in the Qur'an that they are Allah's stewards of creation. This means that they have a responsibility to care for the earth and everything that lives on it. Muslims believe that they have a responsibility to preserve the unity in creation created by God and that if they fail in this duty they may be judged badly at akirah. Many Muslims try to do their bit to help the environment. For example, by being careful and not wasting stuff, 'Allah loves not the wasters'. They will recycle things and maybe not use the car when walking is an option. They may also try to reuse things and give unwanted clothes, books and toys to charity shops. Muhammad said that 'the earth is green and beautiful' and Muslims firmly believe that it is their job to keep it that way.

3 With a partner, discuss the sample answer. Do you think there are other things that the student could have included in their answer?

4 What mark would you give this answer out of 6? Look at the mark scheme in the Introduction on page 7 (AO1). What are the reasons for the mark that you have given?

Practice questions

1   Look at the photograph and answer the following questions.

   (a) Describe **two** different types of pollution.   *(4 marks)*
   (b) Explain Muslim attitudes to pollution. Refer to Muslim teachings and beliefs
       in your answer.   *(6 marks)*

   (c) What does Islam teach about the care of animals?   *(4 marks)*

   (d) 'Muslims should not keep pets.'
       What do you think? Explain your opinion.   *(3 marks)*
   (e) 'Experimenting on live animals is always wrong.'
       What do you think? Give reasons for your answer, showing that you have
       thought about more than one point of view. Refer to Islam in your answer.   *(6 marks)*

5.1   The law and punishment

▊ Lawlessness

In 1954, the British writer William Golding wrote a novel called 'Lord of the Flies'. It tells the story of a group of boys stranded on a deserted tropical island when the plane they were travelling in was shot down in wartime. After an attempt to establish leadership and rules, the community became less and less civilised and partly descended into savagery. The group soon split, with some boys trying to work together to maintain order and to achieve common goals whilst the others were more interested in lawlessness and violence. It is thought that Golding was trying to portray the struggle that exists in the minds of many people. This is the struggle between behaving morally and obeying rules and the instinct to be selfish, ignore morality and conscience and engage in violence.

A   *A scene from Lord of the Flies*

Objectives

Analyse and understand the need for law and punishment.

Key terms

Law: rules in a country that govern how people live.

Crime: the breaking of a state law.

Discussion activities

Imagine that you have been parachuted into a society that did not have any laws. With a partner, discuss what your life would be like. How would you feel?

Study tip

If answering a questions that asks you to say what you think and to explain your opinion, give at least one well developed reason or several simple reasons.

Activities

1   Do you think it is correct to say that people face a struggle between choosing to behave morally and choosing to be selfish and ignore morality? Explain your opinion.

2   'It is easier to behave morally than immorally.' What do you think? Explain your opinion.

Extension activity

Try to read 'Lord of the Flies' or alternatively, watch the film that was made from the book.

The state of living without the authority of **law** is called anarchy. This does not necessarily create chaos and disorder. However, with human nature being as it is, as in 'Lord of the Flies', it is likely to lead to traditional moral values being abandoned in the promotion of selfishness leading to violence.

This is not a state that Muslim ethics could tolerate. Teachings from the *Qur'an* and the *Hadith* make it quite clear that life should be structured and influenced by Allah. This promotes a society that exists and works for the good of everyone.

As it says in Chapter 1, many Muslim countries are ruled by Shari'ah law. This provides a structure intended to establish a fair society. Not all Muslim countries operate Shari'ah law but those that do tend to have a lower crime rate than most other countries. This could be partly due to the harsh punishments given to proven offenders. However, it is also due to the fact that, as Shari'ah law is derived from the *Qur'an* and *Hadith*, it is seen as the will of Allah which Muslims do not wish to break.

links

See pages 10–11 for explanation of Shari'ah law.

B | *A possible result of anarchy*

So why keep the law?

There are two main ways of persuading people to keep the law. As in school, people can either be encouraged by promise of reward or alternatively threatened with punishment. Whilst reward is preferable, there are still some who break the rules and have to be punished.

The reward for keeping the law of the country in which you live is a pleasant society full of people who also keep the law. At least that would be so if everybody wanted life to be like this. However, some choose to break the law and so face punishment. One of the reasons why society imposes punishment is to try and ensure that the offender will keep the law in future. Keeping the law has to be made preferable to breaking the law otherwise there would be more crime.

Muslim teachings are designed to promote a peaceful and fair society where people can freely live their lives in accordance with the teachings of their religion. The existence of crime threatens this so Muslim ethical teachings which are reflected in Shari'ah law are given a high priority. Breaking the law is therefore not an option that most people consider.

Activities

3   In your opinion, thinking about promised reward or threatened punishment, which is most likely to result in an orderly society? Say why.

4   How can keeping the law be made more preferable to breaking the law?

Extension activity

Explain carefully why breaking the law is not an option that most Muslims consider.

Summary

You should now understand some of the reasons why there is a need for law and punishment.

Does it matter what causes crime?

Some people believe that if a crime is committed against an organisation, possibly by committing fraud, there is no real victim. As a result, they think the crime is of less importance than one where there is an obvious victim. However, this notion of a 'victimless' crime is a false one. Every crime has a victim. If an organisation is defrauded out of money, other clients have to pay more to make up the loss. Making false claims to an insurance company increases premiums for everybody else taking out a policy. As every crime does have a victim, it clearly does matter what causes crime; if the causes of crime can be identified, the amount of crime may be reduced.

A The owner of the car is a victim

What causes crime?

For a Muslim, there is one over-riding cause of crime; living without moral guidance. Anybody following the ethical teaching that Islam provides will not be committing crime. So the obvious remedy for preventing crime is to follow the teaching of Allah and Muhammad as revealed in the *Qur'an* and the *Hadith*. Muslims who do this can be confident that Allah will be just in his judgement. However, good as this ideal is, it doesn't always turn out to be so simple. This is because there are other reasons why crimes are committed:

- Some people commit crimes, especially ones that provide financial gain, because they are **greedy**. They want something that they cannot afford, so they either steal the item or the money to buy it.
- Some people blame their offending on **addiction** to illegal drugs. Either they steal to be able to buy drugs or they commit crimes whilst under the influence of drugs. Either way, it is their addiction that is responsible for their crime. The same could be said about those who abuse alcohol.

B People may steal because they have no alternative

- Crimes can be committed by those in **need**. If they are very poor and cannot afford to provide for their family, they may turn to crime to get what they need.

- Psychological **illness** can also cause people to commit crime. Kleptomania is believed to be a psychological problem that causes people to steal. A temporary loss of control can cause some people to commit violent crime, even murder. This could be a crime of passion where, for example, a loved one betrays their partner.

- Many young people who turn to crime do so because of **peer pressure**. They feel that friends put pressure on them to commit crimes. This may apply especially to members of gangs who are encouraged to show their allegiance by committing a crime.

- **Boredom** may lead some people to commit crime. The 'buzz' they get from the crime provides interest and stimulation missing from their life.

- Criminals may feel there is little chance of being caught so they will **get away with** their crime without punishment.

- Crimes of **hate** are some of the most destructive. They are often a result of prejudice. Some Muslims in non-Islamic countries suffer from religious prejudice sometimes called Islamophobia.

C   *Peer pressure may turn some young people to crime*

D   *Hate is a destructive emotion*

activities

Activities

1. Using the words in **bold**, list the eight causes of crime in your order of importance with the one you think is the strongest first and the weakest last. You can add any other causes you can think of.

2. Explain your choices of the strongest and weakest causes.

3. How far do you think that following the ethical teachings of Islam will reduce crime? Give examples and reasons.

∞ links

Look up the definition of the term 'Islamophobia' in the Glossary at the back of this book.

Study tip

If you are asked about the causes of crime in your exam, you will not have to include all eight listed here. Choose some that you can explain best.

Summary

You should now understand some causes of crime.

Types of crime in Muslim thinking

The link between crime and punishment

In Muslim thinking, different types of crime carry different types of punishment. The punishments are designed to protect society by deterring offenders. The harsh nature of the punishment allows the offender to show repentance and seek forgiveness and purification from Allah. This purification removes the need for further punishment in the afterlife.

The law and punishments laid down in the law are designed to protect six issues relating to human life:

- To protect **belief** – no Muslim is allowed to leave the faith and no person, whether Muslim or non-Muslim, must slander the faith.
- To maintain the **honour of women** and to protect them from being harmed, slandered or degraded in any way.
- To keep an **alert mind** – this rules out the use of alcohol or any other drugs which control the mind.
- To protect people's **property**.
- To emphasise the importance of **life** by severely punishing a person who takes life.
- To support the **family** and guarantee identity by forbidding sexual relations outside marriage.

Objectives

Know and understand the link between crime and punishment.

Understand that in Islam there are different types of crime which carry different punishments.

A *Laws and punishments provide protection*

Activities

1. Using the words in **bold**, rank these six issues in your order of importance with the one that you think is most important at the top, and the least important at the bottom.
2. Explain your choice of most and least important.

Discussion activity

With a partner, draft some laws and suggested punishments to uphold one of these six issues. Your teacher may tell you which issue to work on.

Types of crime and punishment

In systems of Islamic law, there are four types of crime which are punished in different ways.

Beliefs and teachings

The woman and the man guilty of adultery or fornication, flog each of them with a hundred stripes: Let not compassion move you in their case.... and those who launch a charge against chaste women, and produce not four witnesses (to support their allegations), flog them with eighty stripes; and reject their evidence ever after.

Qur'an 24:2&4

Unforgivable crimes (Hadud)

This accounts for seven different crimes which cannot be forgiven. Punishments are laid down in the *Qur'an* or the *Hadith*. They are all physical punishments including death. The crimes are: fornication or adultery; making a false accusation against an honourable woman, e.g. that she has committed adultery; theft; drinking alcohol or taking drugs; rebellion against the state; rejection of Islam by Muslims; and highway robbery.

Forgivable crimes (Al-Jynayaat)

These crimes are against the rights of the individual who can then either demand severe punishment as retribution or forgive them and accept 'blood money' in return for a lighter sentence. It is mainly used for bodily harm or murder (when the victim's family have the choice to accept blood money or condemn the murderer to execution).

Community crimes (Al Ta'azir)

These are crimes which affect the community but are not covered by Hadud or Al-Jynayaat. They cover such things as fraud and antisocial behaviour. A judge will give the punishment based upon his learning   of Islamic texts. This is how most crime is dealt with in Islamic countries today.

Crime against the state law (Al-Mukhalafat)

These are crimes against a law the state has enacted. They include offences such as breaking the speed limit or illegal parking. A judge will use his discretion and learning in deciding upon punishment.

B   *Drinking alcohol is classed as an unforgiveable crime*

C   *Speeding is a crime against the state law*

Activities

3   Briefly explain the **four** types of crime in Muslim thinking.

4   'These four types of crime and punishment ensure Muslim countries are mainly crime free.' What do you think? Explain your opinion.

Extension activity

Do you think it is right that a victim or their family can reduce a sentence (often of execution) by accepting blood money? Explain your reasons.

⊂⊃**links**

Look in the Glossary at the back of this book for definitions of the four different types of crime: Hadud, Al-Jynayaat, Al Ta'azir and Al-Mukhalafat.

Summary

You should now know about the link between crime and punishment, and the four types of Islamic crimes and their punishments.

What does punishment achieve?

The law is intended to allow people to live their lives in a society that does not allow people to exploit others or to cause people to live in fear. It also helps to ensure a person can live safely and protects their property. Whenever there is a system of law in place, as there is in every country in the world, there has to be a system of **punishments** to support the law. This allows people who break the law to be punished by those who make and keep the law. Without punishment, there would be less incentive for some people to keep the law.

In some instances, people who do wrong can be seen to be punishing themselves. One such example could be bullying. Those who value and respect other people would not dream of involving themselves in bullying. This is because they realise that it causes unhappiness and would probably make themselves unpopular with others. Those who perhaps do not value or respect other people and treat them badly may find that people either keep well out of their way or are aggressive towards them as a defence mechanism against their bullying. In a sense, unhappiness caused through being unpopular and being isolated by all of their peers, apart from those they intimidate, can be seen as the bully punishing themselves. The same logic could be used for not doing homework.

As regards homework, punishment for not doing it supports the system of setting homework to benefit study. If homework was not important, there would be no justification in punishing people who didn't do it. If there was no punishment, some students would be allowed to disadvantage themselves without the fear of punishment to keep them doing what is right. Of course, fear of punishment is not the main reason why most people complete their homework but it may be for some.

A What's your motivation for doing homework?

Objectives

Understand what punishment is trying to achieve.

Evaluate deterrence as an aim of punishment.

Key terms

Punishment: that which is done to a person because they have broken a law.

Deterrence: to put people off committing crimes. One of the aims of punishment.

Activities

1 Explain how punishment for not doing homework helps to reinforce the importance of homework.

2 What are your reasons for completing or not completing homework?

3 If there was no punishment for not completing homework, would you complete yours? Give reasons for your answer.

◼ Deterrence

Deterrence means to persuade people to keep the law by showing them what will happen to them if they break it. If they see that beating somebody up in the street will probably lead to them spending some time in prison, they may be deterred from committing this crime. They may have been in prison before. Recalling the experience of being locked in a cell for most of the day with no freedom to do what they want to do reinforces that they do not want to return there. This is a very powerful aim because it uses likely punishments as a way of persuading people to keep the law.

Islam takes this aim very seriously. Certain Muslim countries that operate under Shari'ah law use capital punishment (the death penalty) and corporal punishment (physical punishment) for certain offences. These are often carried out in public and large crowds have been known to be attracted by punishments given to some criminals.

Thus punishment becomes an example for others to learn from.

Study tip

When evaluating punishments, it is important to remember their aims.

B   *This offender's hand was amputated to stop him from stealing*

Beliefs and teachings

The woman and the man guilty of adultery or fornication, flog each of them with a hundred stripes ... and let a party of the Believers witness their punishment.

Qur'an 24:2

Activities

4   Explain the theory of how deterrence works.

5   'Making an example of other people is wrong.' Do you agree? Give reasons for your answer, showing that you have thought about more than one point of view.

Summary

You should now have thought about the aim of punishment and in particular deterrence as an aim of punishment.

Discussion activity 🎎

Spend five minutes discussing with a partner whether punishment should become an example for others to learn from.

Protection

Any government has the responsibility to provide protection for their citizens. For this reason, serious offenders are taken out of society and put into prison to protect the rest of society from any future offences they may commit.

More lenient sentences for less serious crimes may also protect others in the future because if they are effective, the offender will not commit any more crimes.

Reformation

For many people, this is the most important aim of punishment but for Muslims it is often seen as less important. However, it is necessary for an offender to seek Allah's forgiveness and to become purified. This is more likely to happen if he or she becomes 'a better person'. The focus of reformation is that whatever punishment is given, it should try to help the offender not to commit further crimes. If a person is in prison, they should be helped to come to terms with what they have done. They should be made to realise why it was wrong and encouraged not to commit any other offence once they are released.

In Britain, if the authorities are satisfied that an offender is reformed, they may be released from prison early on parole. Behaving well in prison is taken as a sign that an offender is reformed. Many Islamic countries do not offer parole. Offenders are required to serve their full sentence. They are expected not to reoffend, more through the deterrence factor of a harsh prison regime rather than through a process of reformation.

Retribution

There is a strong emphasis on retribution in the way Muslims punish offenders. Once an offender is found guilty (and Islamic courts require substantial evidence to prove guilt), their punishment is designed to punish them on behalf of the victim rather than to reform them. There is an opportunity, however, for those wronged by the offender in serious crimes to choose compensation in return for a lighter sentence for the offender. If the wronged person chooses compensation Allah sees this as an act of mercy.

A Society is protected from this offender whilst he is in prison

Beliefs and teachings

We ordained therein for them: 'Life for life, eye for eye, nose for nose, ear for ear, tooth for tooth, and wounds equal for equal.' But if any one remits the retaliation by way of charity, it is an act of atonement for himself.

Qur'an 5:45

However, as Allah created every living thing, and in the case of Shari'ah law, created the law as well, any offence is an offence against him. This makes it serious and worthy of strong punishment.

This emphasis on retribution may contribute to low crime rates in many countries with Shari'ah law. Of course the predominance of Muslims who feel it is their duty to keep Allah's law rather than break it in such countries provides another strong reason for the lower crime rates there.

B   *Prison*

Discussion activity

With a partner or small group, think about and discuss the previous paragraph. Do you think the low crime rate in many Muslim countries is the result of retribution or a duty to keep Allah's law?

Activities

1 Explain what protection, reformation and retribution are.
2 Which of these three aims of punishment do you think is most important? Explain your choice.
3 'Helping an offender is more important than protecting society.' Write a response to this quotation that you would expect a Muslim to give.

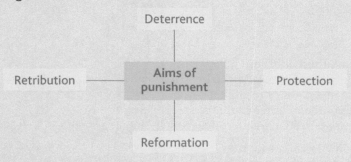

4 Can you think of anymore aims of punishment? What are they?

Study tip

You may see this referred to as revenge. You can use this if you wish to but it is best to use the term in the specification, i.e. retribution.

Summary

You should now know and be able to evaluate three further aims of punishment and Muslim attitudes to these aims.

5.6   A range of punishments

■ Various punishments

It is important to remember that no matter what country you are living in or visiting, if you commit an offence, you are tried and punished by the legal system of that country.

Case study

Despite protesting her innocence, in October 2008, Michelle Palmer was fined £200 for drunkenness and sentenced to three months in jail for having sexual intercourse outside marriage and offending public decency. Her co-accused, fellow Briton Vince Acors, received the same sentence. The offence was committed in Dubai – one of the seven provinces or Emirates that make up the United Arab Emirates (UAE). Over recent years, Dubai City has become a popular destination for wealthy westerners to work and take holidays. However, despite being welcoming to overseas visitors, its laws and punishments are rooted in its Islamic heritage.

The court heard that the couple had been drinking champagne in a five star hotel and later on went to the beach where they were accused of having sex. Whilst drinking alcohol in a private hotel is permitted in Dubai, appearing to be drunk in public is not. In addition, sexual intercourse in public and between unmarried partners are also offences. The couple admitted kissing and cuddling but denied that there was any sexual intercourse.

Their punishments could have been much more severe but it is thought that the sentence was meant to strike a balance between the strict laws that exist in Dubai and the more liberal laws that exist in countries where many visitors to Dubai come from. This case can be seen as a symbol of a culture clash in the UAE between the westerners who are encouraged to visit Dubai and the Arabic legal system that keeps Dubai relatively crime free.

The jail sentence was suspended on appeal and the couple, who are no longer together, were later pardoned and deported back to Britain.

Objectives

Understand that there is a wide range of punishments for offenders that may be dependent on the country in which the offences took place.

A   *Dubai court*

Discussion activity 👥👥👥

1. Given that Michelle Palmer and Vince Acors broke the law in Dubai, was their original punishment fair? Discuss this with a partner and think of some reasons for your opinion. Why do you think they were later pardoned and deported?

It is possible that if the offence had been committed in Britain it *might* not even have been dealt with by a court. However, because Michelle and Vince's alleged offences were committed in a country where the law is much stricter, even though they were not living in that country long-term, their original sentence seems comparatively harsh.

In Britain, compared with punishments in some Muslim countries, some punishments seem quite lenient. Minor first offences are usually punished with a police caution which usually only gets taken into

B   *Vince Acors*

account if further offences are committed. Community service is often a sentence passed by a court to enable the offender to give something back to the community they have offended against. It involves helping out in community projects, for between 40 and 240 hours, spread over several months without receiving any money for doing so. These projects could involve gardening, painting and decorating or, provided the offenders meet certain conditions, working in a charity shop or with a community group.

Fines are often imposed to penalise the offender financially, often for motoring offences such as speeding or for failing to buy certain licences such as a television licence. Prison is reserved for the most serious offences such as murder, crimes involving violence, dishonesty involving large sums of money or repeatedly committing more minor offences. Life sentences are compulsory for murder. However, these sentences usually carry a recommendation from the judge that the offender will be considered for parole (early release from prison but with some conditions imposed) after a certain number of years.

Under no circumstances will the death penalty (capital punishment) or any punishment that causes physical harm to the offender be used in Britain or any other country in the European Community. Indeed in Britain the death penalty was made an illegal punishment in 1965. Despite several campaigns to restore it, it will require a change in British and European law to bring it back. However, it still exists in such countries as China, Saudi Arabia, Iran and some states in the USA.

Key terms

Community service: work which helps the community – sometimes used as a punishment for offenders.

Fine: money paid as punishment for a crime or other offence.

Study tip

If expressing an opinion, try to use reasoning to support your view, rather than arguing from an emotional viewpoint.

Activities

1   Do you think it is right that if a visitor to a different country commits an offence they should be subject to the law and punishment of that country? Explain your reasons.

2   If you were a judge with no rules to obey on sentencing, what punishment would you give for the following offences:

a   Drunkenness

b   Indecent behaviour

c   Driving at 40 mph in a 30 mph area

d   Failure to buy a TV licence

e   Murder

f   Armed robbery

g   Rape

Explain your reasons for each punishment.

3   'The death penalty should be brought back.' What do you think? Explain your opinion.

Discussion activity

2   Put the offences in Activity 2 in order from most serious to least serious. In pairs, discuss how you made your decision, and any differences between your lists.

Extension activity

Should people campaign to change legal systems in other countries that they disagree with? Explain your reasons.

Summary

You should now understand the range of punishments that may apply in Britain or in different countries.

5.7 The death penalty and corporal punishment

Definitions

The death penalty is often known by the term **capital punishment**. Banned in many countries, the death penalty allows offenders found guilty of offences the state regards as very serious to be legally put to death. This can be by lethal injection or the electric chair, as in some states in the US, or hanging, stoning or being shot, in some other parts of the world.

 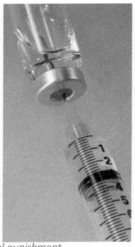 

A *Some methods of capital punishment*

Corporal punishment is different. If somebody receives a sentence of corporal punishment, it means they face a punishment that causes physical pain. Under Shari'ah law, this is usually carried out in the form of being caned, possibly more than a hundred times over the course of several days. Fewer countries use corporal punishment than capital punishment (the death penalty).

The death penalty (capital punishment)

Beliefs and teachings

Take not life, which Allah hath made sacred, except by way of justice and law.

Qur'an 6:151

Under Shari'ah law, the death penalty can be imposed for various offences. As in some non-Muslim countries, murder is punishable by the death penalty, but only if the victim's family rejects the 'blood money' offered to them. In some Muslim countries, other offences also carry the death penalty. These include: insulting Islam; rejecting Islam and converting to a different faith; and adultery (having an affair with another person outside marriage). It is quite rare for such punishments to be carried out in most Muslim countries. However, in some countries that base their criminal code on a strict interpretation of Shari'ah law, they are more common.

Case study

Men stoned to death for adultery but women spared

In two separate cases in Iran, two men were stoned to death in the city of Masshad whilst two women were found not guilty. Both cases involved the accused people allegedly committing adultery.

Details of the stoning are not available but it is thought that three men found guilty of adultery were buried up to their waists in public before having stones thrown at them by volunteers from the people present. One of the three men managed to scramble away and under Muslim law was released from the sentence. The other two were killed. This was the first time in eighteen months that anybody in Iran has faced such a sentence and it is seen as a major setback by those in Iran seeking to outlaw this punishment.

In a separate case, two sisters were freed after their husbands confirmed that film that was thought to show them with other men actually featured two other women who looked similar to them. In August 2007, the sisters had received 99 lashes for an 'illegitimate relationship' and then freed. They were rearrested and sentenced to death by stoning in November 2007 before being freed in January 2009 after a judge ruled there was insufficient evidence for the verdict to be considered safe.

Politicians and campaigners opposed to this form of punishment are hopeful that it could be made illegal within months.

B   *After being flogged, this man was hanged*

Activities

1. Explain your thoughts about one of the two cases outlined in the case study.
2. Why do you think the man who escaped the stoning was allowed to go free?

■ Corporal punishment

Under Shari'ah law, physical punishments are permitted. Many Muslim countries do not use them but some do. In countries such as Saudi Arabia and Iran, it is not uncommon for a thief to have their hand amputated in public by a surgeon. This not only prevents the thief from stealing again but serves as a deterrent to the rest of the population.

Activities

3. In your opinion, do you think a surgeon should agree to amputate the hand of a convicted thief? Give reasons.
4. 'The death penalty and corporal punishment reduce crime.' What do you think? Explain your opinion.

Beliefs and teachings

As to the thief, Male or female, cut off his or her hands: a punishment by way of example, from Allah, for their crime.

Qur'an 5:38

Public floggings are also carried out to inflict physical pain on offenders. However, such punishments are not everyday occurrences because in countries that use them, crime rates tend to be very low. This may be because these public punishments deter potential offenders or because a society based on Muslim teachings is less likely to 'breed criminals'.

Summary

You should now understand the place of capital and corporal punishment in Muslim practice and be able to evaluate whether it should be used.

The importance of Allah in punishment and final judgement

The one true judge

Regardless of how people judge each other and no matter what punishments they give, there is only one true judge who has the ultimate sanction. This one true judge is Allah, who can condemn sinners to an eternity in hell on the Day of Judgement. This is a greater deterrent and a stronger way of protecting society than any punishment that man can impose. Taking away an offender's life by using capital punishment is the greatest sanction people can impose. However, this only hands over the final judgement in the afterlife to Allah, the one true judge.

Objectives

Understand the role of Allah in punishment and final judgement.

Evaluate the importance of this belief.

Key terms

Judgement: God deciding about individual deeds, good and bad, and rewarding or punishing.

A The scales of justice

Beliefs and teachings

They ask, 'When will be the Day of Judgement and Justice?' (It will be) a Day when they will be tried (and tested) over the Fire! 'Taste ye your trial! This is what ye used to ask to be hastened!' As to the Righteous, they will be in the midst of Gardens and Springs, Taking joy in the things which their Lord gives them, because, before then, they lived a good life. They were in the habit of sleeping but little by night, And in the hour of early dawn, they (were found) praying for Forgiveness; And in their wealth and possessions (was remembered) the right of the (needy,) him who asked, and him who (for some reason) was prevented (from asking).

Qur'an 51:12–19

Discussion activity

'Reminding people of God's involvement in punishment after death is the best way to control people's behaviour.' Discuss this statement with a partner. Be prepared to share your conclusion together with your reasons for it with the rest of the class.

Activity

1 Explain what you think these verses from the *Qur'an* mean and how they may influence Muslims in their day-to-day lives.

■ Crime is an offence against the law of Allah

Muslims believe that Allah is involved in the condemnation of the criminal because, in breaking the law, offenders are offending directly against Allah's law. This is because Shari'ah law is believed to have been given or inspired by Allah in order that his people should live in an ethical or moral way. Therefore offending against Shari'ah law is not just wrong. It is considered a sin against Allah which is properly punishable by him. Sins against Allah are put into three categories:

- Shirk – this is being motivated or acting in such a way that suggests equality with Allah. It includes worshipping other gods instead of or alongside Allah and such un-Muslim practices as sorcery and idolatry.
- Zalim – disobeying the rules of Islam and consequently harming the rights of others. This covers offences such as murder, theft and rape.
- Fasiq – a rebel or transgressor which covers areas such as lying, envy and cursing. Someone who is morally corrupt, that is, a person who cares little for morality and behaves in an immoral way.

It is impossible to be a true Muslim (i.e. someone who submits their life to the will of Allah) whilst breaking Allah's law. Indeed breaking the law is an unnatural act. This is because the offender is going against the original nature to do good with which Allah created all human beings.

However, a key belief about Allah is that he will forgive any offender who returns to him in true repentance.

Study tip

Remember, an offence is only considered a sin if it offends against God.

Activities

2 Explain the **three** categories of sins against Allah. Do you think these three categories are a good way of grouping sins? Give your reasons.

3 Explain ways in which Shari'ah law may persuade people to live in an ethical way. You should use ideas learnt throughout this chapter.

4 Why is it thought impossible for a lawbreaker to be a true Muslim?

B   *Shirk, Zalim, Fasiq*

Summary

You should now know and understand more about the role and motivation of Allah in the punishment of offenders. You will have considered whether these Muslim beliefs about Allah and the final judgement after death help people to keep the law.

Justice

Justice is all to do with fairness. If an offender is said to have been dealt with justly, it means they have been through a fair trial. In this trial a knowledgeable judge has listened to evidence from both sides of the case. The judge has then made a judgement based on that evidence without unreasonable favouritism to either side. If the person is found guilty, their punishment should be a just one. Such a punishment reflects the severity of the crime and not feelings for or against the offender.

Beliefs and teachings

O ye who believe! stand out firmly for Allah, as witnesses to fair dealing, and let not the hatred of others to you make you swerve to wrong and depart from justice. Be just: that is next to piety: and fear Allah. For Allah is well-acquainted with all that ye do.

Qur'an 5:8

Shari'ah courts in Islam operate on this basis. Their punishments may seem harsh in some cases but there is a duty upon the courts to reach the right decision after a fair and just trial.

Activities

1. Explain carefully the meaning of the word justice.
2. Look at the quotation from the *Qur'an* 5:8. Do you think that the hatred of others should make a person do wrong and depart from justice? Explain your opinion.

What does the *Qur'an* say?

Beliefs and teachings

Nor can goodness and Evil be equal. Repel (Evil) with what is better: Then will he between whom and thee was hatred become as it were thy friend and intimate!

Qur'an 41:34

This quotation appears to be saying that goodness and evil are not equal. From other teachings throughout Islam, we can assume that Muslims believe that goodness is far more important than evil and that goodness will overcome. A duty for Muslims is to repel evil with what is better, i.e. goodness. In other words, Muslims should do what they can to remove the possibility and influence of evil. Methods of doing so should be good and just. However, these methods could possibly involve violence provided the cause of that violence is the

Objectives

Understand the concepts of justice and forgiveness.

Relate these concepts to Muslim beliefs about crime and punishment.

Key terms

Forgiveness: to pardon a person for something that they have done wrong.

links

Read pages 54–55 for more on Muslim ideas about justice.

Extension activity

If a trial is fair and just, do you think that harsh punishments can be justified? Give reasons for your opinion.

Study tip

This is the only quotation mentioned in the exam syllabus for this chapter. It will therefore help if you learn it because it may be used in a question and expected, if relevant, in an answer.

A *A representation of the struggle between good and evil*

removal of evil and the establishment of justice. If this is the case, the amount of violence used should be just enough to achieve the cause of replacing evil with good. Application of this interpretation can be seen in history wherever Muslims have fought against injustice and evil, believing they have Allah on their side. This could be seen as the lesser jihad.

The quotation in *Qur'an* 41:34 makes it clear that if the instruction to defeat evil and establish goodness is followed, friendship rather than hatred will be the result. This will encourage brotherhood and the achievement of harmony, both of which are key aims in Muslim ethics.

Forgiveness

Muslims do not see punishment as a way for a person to make up for an offence they have committed. Punishment comes from society and is to satisfy the demands of those who are wronged. It is to clearly establish and support the ethical teachings laid down in the faith. Only Allah can truly **forgive** and he will only forgive those who he knows are sorry for what they have done and intend to follow his teachings properly in the future. This is in line with the compassionate and merciful nature of Allah. People should also forgive, and not bear grudges, because that is a just way to establish goodness over evil rather than allowing evil and injustice to grow further.

B *Forgiveness?*

links

For more information on jihad, see Chapter 3.

Discussion activity

Do you think it is right to use violence to remove evil and establish justice? Discuss this with a partner and be prepared to share your ideas with others.

Activities

3   Do you think that defeating evil and establishing goodness will result in friendship rather than hatred?

4   How far do you think punishments establish and support ethical teachings? Give an example to support your opinion.

5   Does forgiveness really establish goodness over evil? Explain your answer.

Summary

You should now understand the concepts of justice and forgiveness and be able to relate these concepts to Muslim teachings on crime and punishment.

5

Crime and punishment – summary

For the examination, you should now be able to:

✔ explain how the Muslim views of law, punishment and forgiveness influence attitudes towards:

- the causes of crime

- the aims of punishment especially deterrence, protection, reformation and retribution

- the impact of punishment on society and the individual

- types of punishment including imprisonment and community service

- corporal punishment and the death penalty (capital punishment)

- the teaching of the *Qur'an* on punishment

- final judgement before Allah

- issues of justice

- the approach to forgiveness

✔ apply relevant Muslim teachings to each topic

✔ give your own opinions supporting them with argument and evidence and discuss issues from different points of view.

Sample answer

1 Write an answer to the following examination question:
Explain Muslim attitudes to corporal punishment. (*4 marks*)

2 Read the following sample answer:

> Muslim attitudes to corporal punishment are very clear. Thieves have their hands cut off and adulterers are stoned to death. This is because they believe that deterring offenders and potential offenders from committing further crimes is important. No one likes pain, so no one wants to be corporally punished.

3 With a partner, discuss the sample answer. Do you think that there are other things that the student could have included in the answer?

4 What mark would you give this answer out of 4? Look at the mark scheme in the Introduction on page 7 (AO1). What are the reasons for the mark you have given?

Practice questions

1   Look at the photograph and answer the following questions.

(a) Give **two** reasons why some people commit crime.   *(4 marks)*

Study tip To gain full marks, you must include two reasons. Including three will not get you extra marks.

(b) 'Deterring people from committing crime is the most important aim of punishment.'
Do you agree? Give reasons for your answer, showing that you have thought about more than one point of view. Refer to Islam in your answer.   *(6 marks)*

Study tip Don't forget to refer to Islam in your answer otherwise you cannot gain more than 3 marks.

(c) Explain, using an example, the meaning of 'corporal punishment'.   *(2 marks)*

Study tip You will get 1 mark for a correct definition and 1 mark for your example.

(d) 'Muslim victims of crime should always forgive offenders.'
Do you agree? Give reasons for your answer, showing that you have thought about more than one point of view.   *(6 marks)*

Study tip Try to make sure your spelling, punctuation and grammar are good enough to make clear what you are saying. Information you present should be expressed coherently.

6 Relationships and lifestyle

The family (1)

What is a family?

A family is the basic social unit of all societies. A nuclear family is made up of parents and children. The extended family includes all other blood relations. The family plays an important role in governing human behaviour. Most societies expect monogamy between couples, that is, only one partner at one time. As a result, the family unit controls sexual behaviour. It is also the place where most people spend a great deal of their time. The family is where children are raised and learn social behaviour so that they may grow up and contribute positively to society. Within the family there is also safety and security for the sick, disabled or elderly.

In Islam, marriage is the foundation for family life. Islam teaches that a man completes half his faith when he marries. It also allows for limited polygamy. This means having more than one wife and is also called 'plural marriage'. The Prophet Muhammad had several wives as this was customary at the time. Today some Islamic countries follow the guidance of the *Qur'an* and permit a man to have up to four wives. However, this is an exception not a rule. The reasons for plural marriage are historically linked to the need to protect women, in particular widows, who were unable to support themselves if their husbands died. In every case, however, a man may only marry additional women if his first wife agrees and he is able to love and support them.

A A Muslim family

Islamic attitudes to the family

In Islam the family is very important. In the *Qur'an* it is made clear that family life was intended by Allah as a place for security and for the sharing of love and companionship. It is not unusual for Muslims to live in extended families, especially when parents become elderly and require care. When a couple marry, it is expected that this will be the beginning of family life together.

Objectives

Understand Islamic attitudes to the family.

Extension activity

Find out more about plural marriage in Islam. Write a report explaining the advantages and disadvantages.

Beliefs and teachings

Marry women of your choice, two, three or four; but if you fear you will be unable to deal justly with them, then only one.

Qur'an 4:3

The role of parents

Within a marriage there are traditionally clearly defined roles for men and women. The *Qur'an* makes clear that men and women are equal. The roles of men and women are complementary and intended to provide a firm and secure foundation for family life. Men are expected to work, provide for their wife and children, and take responsibility for decisions within the home. Women are expected to look after the home and raise children. In the modern world, however, it is not uncommon for both parents to work and share the home responsibilities.

Parents are expected to nurture, love and care for their children. They are to set a good example to their children. Parents are responsible for teaching their children the beliefs and practices of Islam. When a child is born the father will introduce the baby into the faith by whispering the Bismillah in the child's ear. Parents will also ensure other birth ceremonies are performed including Aqiqah and the circumcision of male children.

Parents will teach their children, as they grow and develop, how to pray, keep halal and live a good Muslim life. Parents will often ensure that their children attend a madrassah (Mosque school) and learn to read the *Qur'an*. On Fridays when many men attend the Jumuah prayers, mothers will remain at home with small children and their daughters and lead worship in the home. As their children reach adulthood, parents will often provide guidance and support for their children in finding a suitable marriage partner. In some cases they will actually arrange a marriage for their son or daughter; however, forced marriages are strictly forbidden. In modern times, however, the term 'assisted marriage' is preferred as many Muslim marriages today are love matches.

B   *Mothers have special responsibilities in Islam*

Bismillah – every chapter of the *Qur'an* (except the 9th) begins with the Bismillah which is, 'In the name of God, most Gracious, most Compassionate.'

Aqiqah – means to cut. A few days after birth the Aqiqah ceremony takes place. The head of the Muslim baby is shaved and gifts to charity are made.

Beliefs and teachings

He has created for you mates from amongst your selves, so that you may live in peace with them; and He has put love and mercy between you.

Qur'an 30:12

The prophet said that when a man marries he completes half his faith.

Hadith

The prophet said of mothers, 'Paradise lies at her feet.'

Hadith

links

Find out more about the madrassah on pages 136–137.

Research activity

Using a library or the internet, find out about the rituals performed when a Muslim child is born.

Activities

1. Describe **three** purposes of the family.
2. Explain the role of parents in Islam.
3. 'Being a parent is the most important responsibility a Muslim has.' What do you think? Explain your opinion.

Study tip

When discussing issues such as plural marriage or arranged marriages be sure you can present different points of view.

Summary

You should now know and understand Muslim attitudes to the family and the role of parents.

Children in Islam

Children are a blessing in Islam and parents have a responsibility to raise their children to be good Muslims. The family is especially important for providing a stable environment for their upbringing. The *Qur'an* also makes clear that children have responsibilities too. To be unkind or disrespectful to one's parents is considered a great sin. It is a duty of children to be respectful to their parents and elders. This responsibility extends to when they are adults.

A　*Muslim children have duties and responsibilities*

The teachings of Islam make clear that parents and children have duties and responsibilities to each other.

B

Children have a right to be:	Children have a responsibility to:
nourished, clothed and protected from harm	respect and obey their parents
loved and supported	accept the just discipline of their parents
treated equally to their brothers and sisters	conduct themselves with humility and dignity
provided with an education	care for their parents in their old age.
assisted in making good marriages.	

Objectives

Understand Muslim attitudes to children and the elderly.

Beliefs and teachings

Be kind to your parents, say not to them a word of contempt or repel them, but address them in terms of honour.

Qur'an 17:23

When asked which acts were the most good, the Prophet replied that the first was prayer and the second was to be good and dutiful to one's parents.

Hadith

He, who has no compassion for children or does not give honour to the elderly, is not a believer.

Hadith

Case study

Wajihia's story

My name is Wajihia, I am 15 and I live in an extended family. I have a sister and a brother and we live in a lovely house with my parents and my grandmother. My non-Muslim friends think this is quite unusual and lots of them say there is no way they would have their parents living with them when they are older. I can understand this; it can be difficult at times. My grandmother can be very grumpy and she is always making comments about the way I should behave. She sometimes causes squabbles between Mum and Dad and she needs lots of help, which means that sometimes I have to stay in to care for her if my parents are going out. It also means I have to share a bedroom with my sister! BUT I wouldn't have it any other way. My grandmother helped to bring us up and she is always standing up for me if Mum gets on my case. It's wonderful having someone with so much experience to turn to for love and advice. I think it would be very disrespectful to make her go and live on her own or in an old persons' home. My grandmother deserves the best and that is to be with her family. When I am older I hope that my parents will feel happy to come and live with me and my husband when it is too difficult for them to live on their own.

C　*Wajihia*

Extension activity

Read Wajihia's story. What do you think are the advantages and disadvantages of living in an extended family? Do children have a responsibility to care for their elderly parents?

The elderly

In Islam, old age is an important time in life. For many retired people they have the opportunity to focus on their faith in a way that may have been limited when they were younger. This could have been due to the pressures of working and family life. The mosque is an important community resource for the elderly, providing a meeting place for worship, study and social activities. The elderly are especially respected in Islam for their wisdom and the contribution they have made to the community.

In the family the elderly come before children who should be considerate of their grandparents' needs. Muslims have a responsibility to care for their parents when they become frail and ill. It is therefore unthinkable to a Muslim to place their parents in an old people's home and many Muslim families have their parents living with them. This should never be regarded as a burden; it is an honour to be able to repay one's parents for the love and support they provided one as a child.

D   *An elderly Muslim man recites the names of Allah in the grounds of a mosque*

Beliefs and teachings

Be good to your parents.   *Qur'an* 6:151

May his nose be rubbed in the dust that saw his parents in old age and did not care for them, he will not enter Paradise.   *Hadith*

Those who show the most perfect faith are kindest to their families.   *Hadith*

Activities

1   Explain the duties and responsibilities of Muslim children.

2   What do the *Qur'an* and the *Hadith* teach about family life?

3   Explain Muslim attitudes to the elderly.

4   'Caring for the elderly at home is not always the best option in the modern world.' Do you agree? Give reasons for your answer showing that you have thought about more than one point of view. Refer to Islam in your answer.

Study tip

Your responses to evaluation questions will be improved by showing awareness of wider issues. In this sample evaluation question (Activity 4), you should refer to alternative ways of caring for the elderly other than in the home.

Summary

You should now know and understand Muslim attitudes to children and the elderly.

Sexuality

For most people sex is an important part of life. Puberty is regarded as a major turning point and marks the transition from a child to an adult. It includes physical and psychological development. It is natural to start to have an interest in sex and relationships. Human sexuality is complex and society reflects this in its expectations and attitudes. Heterosexual relationships between men and women are regarded as the normal pattern of behaviour. Some people are drawn to homosexual relationships and share loving partnerships with someone of the same sex. In all societies there are laws governing the relationships between people.

Islamic attitudes to sexuality

In Islam, sex is accepted as part of being human. It is not considered to be wrong or unhealthy. It is also recognised that sex is for pleasure. Human beings are capable of regulating their sexual behaviour unlike other species of animal. The *Qur'an* says that celibacy, choosing not to marry and have sexual relations, is wrong. The Muslim way of life has an expectation that a man will marry and raise a family. Islam regards sexual relationships between a husband and wife as healthy and a source of blessing from God. This is the only permitted form of sexual relationship.

There are many *Hadith* referring to issues relating to human sexuality. The Prophet provided Muslims with guidance through his responses to many questions. Marriage is intended for companionship and tenderness. The intimacy between a husband and wife is for mutual sharing and satisfaction of desires. Islam does not forbid the use of some forms of contraception, recognising that sex has other purposes than reproduction. Sexual dissatisfaction is considered to be legal grounds for either a man or a woman to seek a divorce.

Sex outside marriage

Islam forbids sexual relations before marriage and outside marriage. Sexual pleasure is something that should not be pursued since this detracts from the dignity of the individuals involved. Sexual responsibility includes moral considerations. When morality is ignored, sex can result in grave consequences for individuals and society. Children have a right to be born into a stable loving home, knowing their mother and father. Sexual promiscuity can lead to other evils such as rape, deception and prostitution. Adultery is strictly forbidden and in some Islamic countries is punished with flogging and even death.

Muslims are encouraged to avoid circumstances which could potentially result in temptation to commit sexual sins. Muslims

Objectives

Understand Muslim attitudes to human sexuality.

Key terms

Heterosexual relationship: a sexual relationship with someone of the opposite sex.

Adultery: sex outside marriage where one or both of the couple are already married to someone else.

A Dating is part of many young people's lives

∞ links

Read Chapter 5 for more on the punishment for adultery in some Islamic countries.

should not 'date' although it is allowed to meet with a potential marriage partner in strictly controlled circumstances. The Prophet encouraged the practice of bride and groom meeting before marriage with a chaperone so that they could begin to develop feelings of love and companionship before their marriage. Muslims should also practise modesty in their dress and exercise self-control in their behaviour. Some Muslim women choose to wear a hijab covering their hair when in public. Others may choose to wear a full body covering called a burqa.

B *A Muslim woman wearing a hijab*

Discussion activity

Compare images of women in traditional Muslim dress with those in western dress. Discuss the advantages and disadvantages of having a dress code.

Beliefs and teachings

Let no man be in privacy with a woman who is not lawful to him, or Satan will be a third.

Hadith

When a husband and wife share intimacy it is rewarded and a blessing from Allah.

Hadith

Nor come nigh to adultery, it is a shameful deed.

Qur'an 17:32

Young people, whoever among you can marry, should marry because it helps you lower your gaze and guard your modesty.

Hadith

Activities

1 What is meant by the term sexuality?
2 What does Islam teach about sex outside of marriage?
3 Explain Muslim attitudes to human sexuality.
4 'There is nothing wrong with dating.' What do you think? Explain your opinion.

Extension activity

Interview some of your family and friends on their views about sex before marriage and/or read some articles on this subject in teenage magazines. Compare the responses with religious teachings on this issue. Write a newspaper report on different attitudes to sex before marriage.

C *Some Muslim women choose to wear a burqa*

Study tip

When you use a quotation in an examination remember to explain how it helped answer the question.

Summary

You should now know and understand Muslim attitudes to human sexuality.

Islamic attitudes to homosexuality

Homosexuality is the term used to describe sexual attraction to the same sex. Islam makes clear that sexual relationships are intended to take place within marriage only. It also expressly forbids any sexual activity which is illegal or frowned upon. Islam recognises that people are capable of many different forms of sexual expression and orientation which demonstrates the uniqueness of God's creation. Sex for human beings is not simply an instinctive response to the need to reproduce. However, the potential for such behaviour does not make it right. Homosexuality is considered to be against the natural law instituted by Allah and so all homosexual relationships are wrong.

The *Qur'an* and the *Hadith* make it clear that people with such desires should control their instincts and not violate the laws of God. Practising homosexuality is considered a crime and there are severe penalties. In practice, however, to be convicted, a person must either confess or there must be at least four eyewitnesses present at the time of the offence. This means that it is unlikely that these individuals would be punished on earth; they will, however, have to answer for their actions on the Day of Judgement.

A *Same sex relationships are forbidden in Islam*

Beliefs and teachings

If women are guilty of lewdness, take the evidence of four (reliable) witnesses from among you, against them … confine them to their homes until death or Allah ordain for them some other way.

Qur'an 4:15

If two men are guilty of lewdness punish them both. If they repent and amend, leave them alone for Allah is … Most Merciful.

Qur'an

'Will you approach males and leave those whom Allah has created for you to be your mates? You are a people transgressing all limits.'

Qur'an 26:165–166

Islamic attitudes to the age of consent

It is recognised that sexual relationships are complex and involve more than just a physical relationship. Sexual maturity also involves emotional and psychological well-being. The onset of puberty may mean the body is ready for sexual activity, but it does not necessarily mean the individual is ready. The term 'age of consent' refers to the age at which a person is considered old enough to legally and freely enter into a sexual relationship. Most countries recognise the need to protect children and have laws stating the age of consent for sexual intercourse. Most state the age of consent as 15 or 16 but there are differences and this age can be higher or lower.

In Islam there is no specified age of consent within the teachings. Sexual relations should only take place within marriage. Also, responsible parenting would require Muslims to make marriage arrangements only when they feel that their children are ready to enter into such a commitment. Islam would say that this should conform to the laws of the country in which they are living.

In Muslim countries there is variation in the legally defined age of consent. Some countries such as Iran and the Yemen do not specify an age but they do have a requirement for the couple to be married. There are also differences in some countries between the legal age of consent for men and women. This usually gives a younger age for women since girls enter puberty earlier than boys. There are Muslim and non-Muslim countries which have laws stating that there is no legal age of consent for homosexuality; it is against the law.

B   *In Islam there is no specified age of consent within the teachings. Sexual relations should only take place with marriage*

Activities

1   Explain these terms:
a   homosexuality
b   age of consent.

2   Explain **two** reasons why Islam considers homosexuality to be wrong.

3   Why do you think it is important to have a legal age of consent?

4   'Religion should not try to control human sexuality.' Do you agree? Give reasons for your answer showing that you have thought about more than one point of view. Refer to Islam in your answer.

Research activity

Find out about assisted marriages in Islam. Write a leaflet explaining the arguments for and against parental involvement in the choosing of a marriage partner. Make clear the difference between assisted marriages and arranged marriages.

Summary

You should now understand about Muslim attitudes to homosexuality and the age of consent.

What are legal drugs?

A drug is any substance that affects the mind or body. A legal drug is one that is not forbidden by the law. Drugs are used for medical and social reasons. When a drug is prescribed by a doctor it is obviously intended to cure illness or alleviate pain. Few would object to the use of these drugs as the intention is good. Drugs such as alcohol and tobacco are also legal in the UK and are sold for adult use. These drugs are taken socially for pleasure. However, there are issues arising out of the use of these drugs because they can also have damaging effects on the individual, their families and society.

Muslim attitudes to legal drugs

Prescribed drugs

Islam teaches that Muslims should respect their bodies as they are a gift from God. It also teaches that science and medicine are worthwhile professions and Allah has given people the intellect to research and develop for the good of humanity. Muslim doctors swear an oath to preserve life and strive to do their best for all people as an act of devotion to God. It is acceptable for Muslims to use drugs if the intention is to cure illness or relieve pain. **Prescribed drugs** and over-the-counter medicines are therefore permitted.

> **Beliefs and teachings**
>
> If any one saved a life, it would be as if he saved the life of the whole people.
>
> *Qur'an* 5:32
>
> Allah has not created any disease, whose cure He has not prescribed.
>
> *Hadith*

Tobacco

Tobacco is a legally available drug used by over 1 billion people worldwide. It can be smoked, chewed or sniffed. The tobacco industry is worth billions of dollars and is an important part of the economy of a number of economically developed and developing countries. It contains a substance called nicotine which is very addictive. However, we now know that it is also extremely harmful. In the short term, tobacco has unpleasant effects on the user such as the smell, staining of hands and teeth, bad breath and poor skin. In the long term, smoking in particular can lead to cancer, heart disease, emphysema and early death.

Islam does not directly forbid the use of tobacco and it is not mentioned in the *Qur'an*. If a Muslim chooses to smoke it is a matter of personal conscience. However, the teachings would suggest that it is a bad habit that should be considered haram. Islam strictly forbids anything which causes harm to oneself or others. When someone smokes, other people also breathe in the toxins from their cigarette,

Objectives

Understand Muslim attitudes to prescribed drugs and tobacco.

Key terms

Prescribed drugs: drugs which are legal, obtained on written instruction of a doctor.

A   *Medicine is considered a noble profession in Islam*

B   *Smoking causes lung cancer*

cigar or pipe; this is called passive smoking. The effects of smoking and passive smoking are now proven to have harmful effects and many Muslims would agree that smoking is wrong for this reason alone. Smoking is also a costly habit and the money wasted could be used for more positive purposes. Most Muslims would agree that people should give up and, for a smoker who is a Muslim, this would be an example of personal jihad. During the month of Ramadan smoking is not permitted during daylight hours.

∞ links

See pages 58–59 for more on jihad.

Beliefs and teachings

Make not your own hands contribute to (your) destruction.

Qur'an 2:195

Squander not your wealth.

Qur'an 17:26

Study tip

When asked to explain attitudes it is helpful to include quotations from the religious teachings.

Activities

1 What is a drug?

2 Explain Muslim attitudes to the use of prescribed drugs.

3 Explain Muslim teaching about tobacco.

4 'A Muslim should never smoke.' What do you think? Explain your opinion.

Extension activity

Use the internet to find copies of the Hippocratic Oath and the Oath of a Muslim Physician. Compare the two.

My name is Kabir and I have recently given up smoking. I started when I was at school like a lot of my friends but it wasn't too long before I was hooked. You never really think about how much harm it does to your body when you're young and healthy or what it costs. Anyway when I got married my wife used to nag me about it because she said it made the house smell and when the children arrived, she made me go outside for a smoke. I had tried to give up before but last Ramadan I finally succeeded. Islam doesn't forbid smoking, but it does teach me that I should care for my body and, during the fast, smoking during daylight hours is not allowed. I decided that like other temptations, I should strive not to give in to it at all, like a personal jihad. I have now been smoke free for a year and feel so much better. My sense of smell and sense of taste have returned and I have lots more energy. My wife has been a great support and says I look younger than ever. With the savings I have made, we are all going on a special family holiday this year to visit relatives in Pakistan.

C Kabir

Case study

Activity

5 Read the case study. What are the advantages of quitting smoking? How did Kabir's Muslim beliefs help him to give up smoking?

Summary

You should now know about Muslim attitudes to prescribed drugs and tobacco.

6.6   Legal drugs (2)

■ Alcohol

Alcohol is a legal drug in most parts of the world. People have been fermenting wines, spirits and beers for centuries. For many people, alcohol is part of everyday life and in the UK many adults regularly drink at home and out socialising. Alcohol is available from many sources including supermarkets, pubs, clubs and restaurants. Many people would probably say that there is nothing wrong with drinking in moderation.

The effects of alcohol

People are affected by alcohol in different ways. Many people would say that they drink because they enjoy the effects of feeling happy and relaxed as well as the actual taste of the drink. However, alcohol has a depressant effect on the body. It slows down brain activity and reflexes; this is why people are more prone to having accidents when they are drunk. It can also cause personality changes. People can become more aggressive or less inhibited, leading them to do things they would not normally do. Long-term abuse of alcohol can lead to addiction. Alcoholics are more likely to die from liver disease and the impact of their drinking on family life can be devastating.

A *Alcohol is widely available in the UK*

■ Muslim attitudes to alcohol

In Islam, alcohol is khamr, which means poison. It is strictly haram, which means that it is forbidden for Muslims to drink. At the time of the Prophet, many people drank and the harmful effects of drunkenness were seen in society. Over time a complete ban on alcohol was introduced. The *Qur'an* makes clear that drinking is a sin and that, even though there are benefits for some, the sin is far greater. Alcohol is regarded as a temptation of the devil to deceive people away from striving in the path of Allah. If a Muslim does drink, their prayers will not be received for 40 days.

Drinking alcohol affects the mind and body. Muslims should not come to worship under the influence of any drug. It would be impossible to perform salah (prayer) five times a day if a person was drinking. Muslims are also told to respect their bodies as gifts from God and alcohol abuse is very damaging. The social effects of drinking should also be considered. Muslims have responsibilities to their families and community. When under the influence of alcohol, a person is not able to fulfil these responsibilities. There is also a danger that they may commit immoral and sinful acts because they are not in their right mind.

Beliefs and teachings

They ask thee concerning wine and gambling. Say: 'In them is great sin and some profit for men; but the sin is greater than the profit.'

Qur'an 2:219

Intoxicants and gambling ... of Satan's handiwork.

Qur'an 5:90

Alcohol is not a medicine but a disease.

Hadith

The evils of alcohol

A man was told he must do one of the following: tear the *Qur'an*, kill a child, worship an idol, drink wine or sleep with a woman. He decided that to drink the wine would be the lesser sin. So he became drunk on the wine and then slept with the woman, killed the child, tore the *Qur'an* and bowed in worship to an idol.

Case study

Activity

1 Read the case study. What does the story teach about the dangers of alcohol?

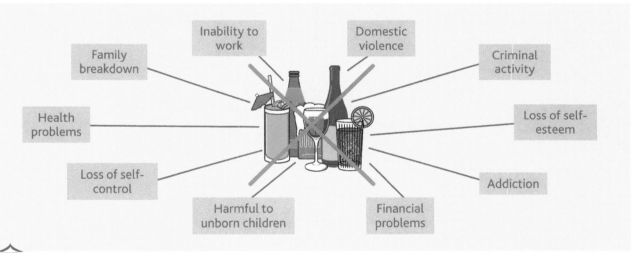

B *The possible effects of alcohol abuse*

Activities

2 Explain why some people drink alcohol.

3 What do the terms khamr and haram mean?

4 What does Islam teach about alcohol use?

5 Explain **three** reasons why Muslims are not allowed to drink alcohol.

6 'Drinking alcohol is the worst sin a Muslim could commit.' Do you agree? Give reasons for your answer showing that you have thought about more than one point of view.

Study tip

Some evaluation questions will be worth 6 marks. In these questions you need to make sure that you give some reasons or arguments that agree with the statement and some which support another point of view.

Summary

You should now know and understand about Muslim attitudes to alcohol.

6.7 Illegal drugs

What are illegal drugs?

Illegal drugs are those that are banned by the government of a country. They are drugs that are considered to be especially harmful to the individual and society. They include drugs such as heroin, cocaine, ecstasy, amphetamines and marijuana (cannabis). In the UK, illegal drugs are categorised depending upon their effects. Anyone found in possession of or trading these drugs is committing a criminal offence. Punishments range from fines to long terms in prison. In some Muslim countries, alcohol is also classed as an illegal drug.

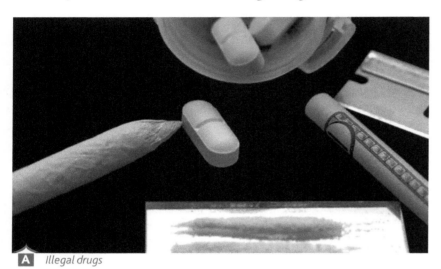

A *Illegal drugs*

Why use illegal drugs?

People who use illegal drugs often do so for the same reasons that many people use legal drugs such as alcohol. Amongst young people, drug taking is often associated with peer pressure and the desire to rebel. Drugs are part of popular culture and some people see nothing wrong with experimenting and enjoy the effects of the drugs they take. However, many illegal drugs are highly addictive and it does not take long for the user to become dependent. When this happens, there can be devastating consequences.

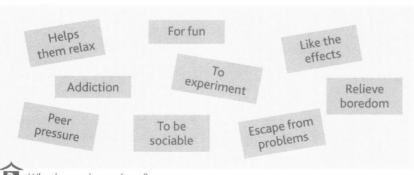

Helps them relax

For fun

Like the effects

Addiction

To experiment

Relieve boredom

Peer pressure

To be sociable

Escape from problems

B *Why do people use drugs?*

Muslim attitudes to illegal drugs

Muslim teaching is clear in its condemnation of drug abuse. Harmful narcotics are khamr because they cloud the mind and judgement. The effects of these drugs mean that it is impossible to be in a state of Taqwa, meaning God-consciousness. A Muslim should always be aware of the will of Allah and should strive to live as Allah has ordained.

Muslims believe that life is a gift from God that is to be cherished. It would be wrong to take any form of narcotic because it is harmful to the body and mind. Muslims are told they must not contribute to their own destruction and using illegal drugs is potentially life threatening. Muslims also believe that they will be judged on how they have lived their life on earth. The intentions of their actions must be pure. The use of illegal drugs could never be considered as having pure intentions. Their use is for selfish pleasures or to escape from the pressures of the real world. When asked to rule on the use of hashish, a Muslim scholar declared it to be haram because its effects could be compared to those of alcohol. A Muslim must strive in the path of Allah and this means facing up to problems and difficulties, not trying to avoid them with mind-altering drugs.

Drug taking is also seen as wrong because of the effects it has on family life and society. Addiction harms families because the user wastes money on a selfish pleasure. The effects of the drug on the user's personality can also cause conflict and distress. Muslims are expected to contribute positively to their communities and be respectful of the law. An addict would find it difficult to participate in society and could not take a full part in family life. Indeed, their unpredictability, mood swings and antisocial behaviour may cause upset and great anxiety within their immediate family. Drug taking sets a poor example to others. The punishment for using drugs in some Islamic countries is a public flogging. However, Muslims would agree that it is important to help addicts overcome their addiction. This is because they believe they should show compassion and mercy for all who are suffering.

Beliefs and teachings

Satan's plan is to excite enmity and hatred between you with intoxicants and gambling.

Qur'an 5:91

Allah has forbidden paradise for the habitual drunkard, one disobedient to parents and a husband who establishes impurity in his family.

Hadith

Activities

1 What are illegal drugs?
2 Why do you think some drugs are illegal?
3 Explain **three** reasons why someone might use illegal drugs.
4 Explain Muslim attitudes to the use of illegal drugs.
5 'A Muslim should never use drugs.' Do you agree? Give reasons for your answer, showing that you have thought about more than one point of view.

links

'Striving in the path of Allah' is covered on pages 58–59.

Research activity

Find out about the work of one drug rehabilitation programme. Write a report based on your findings.

Extension activity

Write a newspaper article on the damaging effects of illegal drug use on family life.

Study tip

When giving reasons in evaluation questions, use examples to illustrate the points that you make. This shows the examiner that you understand the issue you are explaining.

Summary

You should now know and understand Muslim attitudes to the use of illegal drugs.

6.8 Gambling

What is gambling?

Gambling is any activity that involves games of chance, where the outcome is not certainly known. It usually involves a wager or bet for money. For example, a person might think that horse number 2 is going to win a race so they then place money on that prediction. If they are right they get their money back plus more as winnings. There are lots of different types of gambling that are legal in the UK. One of the most widely played games is Lotto. This is a national gambling game based on predicting six numbers. If chosen correctly, the winner could win millions of pounds for a £1 bet.

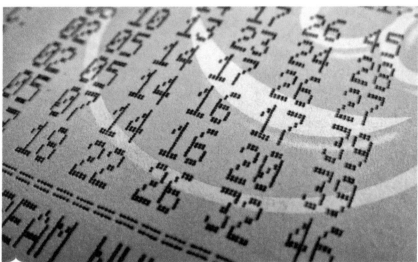

Why do people gamble?

There are many reasons why people may gamble. Some people enjoy the games and consider them to be harmless fun. Many gambling games are associated with the hobbies and interests people have such as horses, card games and sport. For others the games may be associated with socialising such as a night at bingo or an evening in a casino. Gambling can also be a routine such as playing the same numbers on the Lotto. Most people would probably say that they enjoy the thrill of not knowing the outcome and of course, they are especially excited if they win. For some, gambling can become an addiction and this can lead to many problems.

Like any addiction, gambling can have a damaging effect on the individual and their families. It is not difficult to find ways to gamble and addicts can find themselves in serious debt. This places them under immense strain that affects their personality, their relationships and their working life. The pressures of debt can lead to mental health problems such as depression. Being unable to stop gambling can mean members of the family have to go without essentials. Also, the stress on relationships can lead to marital breakdown, loss of job and homelessness.

Muslim attitudes to gambling

The *Qur'an* refers to gambling alongside alcohol as a tool of Satan to tempt believers from the true path of Allah. It is therefore haram and strictly forbidden for a Muslim to gamble. In Arabic the root of the word to gamble means 'easy' or 'without effort'. Islam teaches that money should be earned and not wasted. Gambling makes a person dependent on luck and there can be no security or honesty in obtaining money this way. It is also money won at the expense of someone else's loss. Property in Islam should be fairly traded, so to take another person's wealth by 'winning' would be wrong.

Islam is also concerned with the negative effects that gambling has on the person and society. Gambling causes bitterness and hatred between people because inevitably there are winners and losers. When addicted to gambling a person cannot fulfil their responsibilities to Allah, their families and their communities. Addiction to gambling causes the addict to lose sight of true values because they are more concerned with selfish thrills. In some Muslim countries, the penalty for gambling is a public flogging.

B *Gambling can become addictive*

Beliefs and teachings

When they ask about drinking and gambling say, 'There is great harm in both, though there are benefits for some, the sin outweighs the benefit.'

Qur'an 2:219

Satan's plan is to excite enmity and hatred between you with intoxicants and gambling, and hinder you from remembering Allah and from prayer.

Qur'an 5:91

Activities

1 What is gambling?

2 Explain **three** reasons why some people gamble.

3 Explain why Islam forbids gambling. Refer to teachings in your answer.

4 'A parent addicted to gambling is the worst thing that could happen in a family.' Do you agree? Give reasons for your answer showing that you have thought about more than one point of view. Refer to Muslim teaching in your answer.

Study tip

When explaining the effects of issues like gambling, remember to talk about the effects on the person, their family and society.

Extension activity

Find out about the causes supported by Lotto. Write a report on the advantages and disadvantages this has for charities. Include a response from a Muslim point of view. This should explain why Muslims believe gambling is wrong and alternative ways that charities could be supported.

Summary

You should now know and understand about Muslim attitudes to gambling.

6.9   Usury

What is usury?

The term usury originally meant the charging of interest on a loan and was considered by many to be immoral. During the Middle Ages as trade and commerce increased, the lending of money became an important industry. The laws of many countries were changed to make it legal to charge reasonable interest on a loan. Contracts were made between money lenders and borrowers, who agreed to pay back more than they had loaned. As a result, the lender could make a profit from the service they provided. Today the term usury has come to mean the charging of excessive or unreasonable interest.

In the modern world, it is common for people to borrow money to meet their immediate financial needs. Buying a house, for example, can cost hundreds of thousands of pounds. Most people need to take out a mortgage to pay for the house. This is a special type of loan where, if the borrower fails to repay the loan, the lender can take possession of the property it was used to purchase.

Key terms

Usury: the act of loaning money with excessive interest.

A   *Buying on credit has become part of modern living*

Lending money is big business. People today routinely take out loans for cars, home improvements, holidays and even weddings! Added to this are the pressures to 'buy now, pay later'. Many companies offer a range of credit services where people buy goods by paying a fixed sum of money each month. The use of credit cards is widespread. All these services allow the shopper to have the goods now but they will have to pay more for the product in the end. This is because they will pay interest on the loan they have received.

What is wrong with borrowing money?

Most people would agree that there is a need to be able to borrow money sometimes. However, there are also many potential problems. People can easily get into situations where they cannot afford to pay back what they have borrowed. This can put people under immense strain resulting in ill health. This can complicate matters further if they become unable to work and earn money. The pressures of debt can also be devastating on families. People can find themselves in situations where they cannot afford to pay for the basic necessities for their family and marriages can break down. Debt may also lead to desperate actions such as crime and even suicide. In the modern world, the burden of debt also has an impact on the global economy. Over-lending and interest are partly responsible for issues such as poverty, famine and recession.

Muslim attitudes to usury

In Islam the term riba means usury and it is strictly forbidden in Islamic law. The *Qur'an* makes several references to it and stresses that it is unjust. Those that practise riba are giving in to Satan's temptation and they will be punished severely in the afterlife. If someone is in need, it is more compassionate and just to give to charity; making money out of someone who is in need is very wrong. The same is true of trade. Muslims are expected to trade fairly. To charge more for goods by allowing someone to pay later with interest is wrong.

Islam would also look at the motivation behind wanting to buy material goods before they could be afforded. Muslims should not be extravagant and wasteful, and Islam warns against 'showing off'. It is not wrong to be rich; the *Hadith* say that wealth is one way Allah chooses to bless some. However, desiring possessions and getting into debt to have them leads someone away from their true path to serve God.

B   *Most people need a mortgage to buy a home*

Beliefs and teachings

Devour not usury, doubled and multiplied, but fear Allah, that ye may (really) prosper.

Qur'an 3:130

They took usury though they were forbidden....We have prepared for … them a grievous punishment.

Qur'an 4:161

The riba that is practised to increase some people's wealth does not gain anything from God. But if you give to charity, these are the people who will receive reward.

Qur'an 30:39

Research activity

Use an internet search to find out about Muslim mortgages. How do they differ from traditional mortgages? How do they meet the needs of Muslim lenders and borrowers?

Activities

1   What is usury?

2   Explain **two** reasons why someone might need to borrow money.

3   What problems can be caused by borrowing money?

4   Explain Muslim teaching about usury.

5   'There is nothing wrong with charging interest on a loan.' Do you agree? Give reasons for your answer showing that you have thought about more than one point of view. Refer to Islam in your answer.

Summary

You should now know and understand about Muslim attitudes to usury.

6.10 Islamic schools

Islam and education

For Muslims, acquiring knowledge is a sacred duty and is essential to the good practice of Islam. Learning can help someone become closer to God because it gives them understanding of Allah's will for them. It is a form of worship because without knowledge a Muslim would be unable to strive in the path of Allah. Ignorance can lead to temptation and immorality whereas knowledge helps a Muslim to live correctly. Knowledge enables Muslims to act justly and promote positive values and the message of Islam.

Early Muslim rulers recognised the need for children to be educated and by 900 CE most mosques included a madrassah that provided primary education for boys and girls. Children were taught to read and write the *Qur'an*. Larger schools also provided further education and subjects such as maths, science, history, law and theology were taught to those who wanted more advanced studies. This enabled Muslim civilisations to grow and develop. In medicine, for example, the practices of Arab doctors contributed to the development of many medical procedures still used today.

Objectives

Understand Muslim attitudes to education.

Understand the role and importance of Islamic schools.

links

'Striving in the path of Allah' is covered on pages 58–59.

Beliefs and teachings

Allah grants wisdom to who he pleases and he to whom is granted wisdom receives an overflowing benefit.
Qur'an 2:26

Anyone who searches for knowledge, God will make easy for him the way to paradise.
Hadith

A single scholar is more formidable against Satan than a thousand devout persons.
Hadith

A   *Muslim children reciting the Qur'an in a madrassah*

Madrassah

Madrassah is a term used to apply to any school. Mosques always have a madrassah and an important function of this is to teach children about the *Qur'an* and how to live as a Muslim. In the UK, a madrassah often holds classes for children every evening and at weekends. Boys and girls both attend lessons from the age of five until their teens. Classes are often led by community leaders such as the Imam. Part of his responsibility is to provide education in Islam for children and adults.

Islamic schools

The madrassah provides for religious education but, increasingly in the UK, the Muslim community has called for Muslim state schools to be provided. Islam is a complete way of life and education is expected to be broader than just religious studies. In the modern world, it can be difficult to combine a secular education with the values and practices of Islam. For example, there have been cases where Muslim girls are prevented from wearing the hijab. School meals may not provide halal food. Islam has strict guidelines on the interaction between males and females. Some Muslim parents are concerned when schools do not provide separate classes for things like PE and sex education. Consequently some parents feel there should be an option for their children to attend a state faith school which incorporates Muslim teachings and values.

B   *Should the UK provide faith schools for Muslims?*

Reasons for	Reasons against
■ Parents should have a right to choose an appropriate education for their children.	■ Faith schools can be seen as divisive in a community.
■ There are many faith schools for Christians. So there should be equality of provision.	■ The school system already offers a range of choices for parents.
■ A faith school can provide more than just a secular education.	■ Many schools have adapted to take account of the needs of children from different faith backgrounds.
■ Current faith schools provide an excellent standard of education.	■ Religious practice should be taught at home and in holy buildings, not schools.
■ Muslims contribute fully to the economy; parents should not have to pay privately for appropriate education.	■ Education funding should be used for more important needs.

   Education is considered highly important

Discussion activity ■■■

Look at Table **B**. Can you think of any other reasons for and against having faith schools? Discuss these with a partner.

Activities

1   Why is education considered to be important in Islam?

2   Describe the role of the madrassah in the Muslim community.

3   Explain **two** reasons why some people would support faith schools.

4   Explain **two** reasons why some people would disagree with faith schools.

5   'Faith schools are not necessary.' What do you think? Explain your opinion.

Extension activity

Write a diary for a Muslim student in which they describe the difference between their day at school and their studies in the madrassah.

Research activity

There are now a number of Muslim faith schools in the UK. Use the internet to find out about their philosophy and curriculum. How do they differ from your school? If you attend a faith school, compare your school with a non-faith school.

Study tip

Make sure you understand the command words used in exam questions. These are the instructions such as describe, outline, explain.

Summary

You should now understand the importance of education for Muslims and the role of Islamic schools.

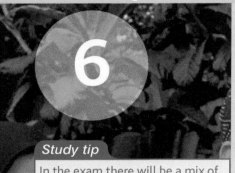

6

Relationships and lifestyle – summary

For the examination your should now be able to:

✓ show an understanding of how Muslim beliefs, law and the principles of commitment and responsibility influence Muslim attitudes to:

- the importance of the family: children, the role of parents and the elderly
- human sexuality and sexual relationships (heterosexual and homosexual)
- the legal age of consent for sexual intercourse
- alcohol, tobacco, prescribed drugs, illegal drugs
- the effects and impact of drug use on individuals and others
- gambling
- usury (charging interest on money loaned)
- the role of Islamic schools.

Sample answer

1 Write an answer to the following examination question:

'Gambling is always wrong.'
Do you agree? Give reasons for your answer, showing that you have thought about more than one point of view. Refer to Islam in your answer. (*6 marks*)

2 Read the following sample answer:

> In Islam this is always true. Muslims believe that gambling is wrong because it is the work of Satan. The Qur'an says that Satan has made up these games of chance to test us and make hatred between people. Some people think that gambling is just a bit of harmless fun. They say that games like bingo and Lotto do not really do any harm and that they can help people. Lotto has made millions of pounds for charities and so this must be a good thing. Islam would not agree because gambling is a waste of money. Most people do not win when they gamble and if they become addicted to it, they could get into lots of money troubles. This would be really terrible for their families because they might not be able to afford to buy essentials like food and nice clothes.

3 With a partner, discuss the sample answer. Do you think there are other things that the student could have included in their answer?

4 What mark would you give this answer out of 6? Look at the mark scheme in the Introduction on page 7 (AO2). What are the reasons for the mark that you have given?

Practice questions

1   Look at the photograph and answer the following questions.

(a) Describe the roles and responsibilities of the members of a Muslim family.   *(6 marks)*

Study tip   In this question you can refer to parents, children and the extended family.

(b) 'Caring for your family is more important than following a religion.'
Do you agree? Give reasons for your answer, showing that you have
thought about more than one point of view. Refer to Islam in your answer.   *(6 marks)*

(c) Explain Muslim attitudes to the use of alcohol and tobacco.   *(6 marks)*

Study tip   You must refer to Muslim attitudes to both alcohol **and** tobacco to achieve full marks. If you only refer to one, you cannot gain full credit even if you write lots of detail.

(d) 'It is too hard to live by the rules of Islam in the world today.'
How far do you agree? Give reasons for your answer, showing that you have
thought about more than one point of view.   *(6 marks)*

Study tip   In Part B of the exam you will have a choice of two questions from different topics. These questions will require you to answer in detail. Make sure you read both of the question choices carefully and answer the one that you feel most confident about.

Glossary

A

Abortion: the deliberate termination (ending) of a pregnancy, usually before the foetus is twenty-four weeks old.

Adultery: sex outside marriage where one or both of the couple are already married to someone else.

Aid: to help or assist people in need, usually by gifts or money. Most people think of this as donating to charities that provide help to the poor, particularly in the developing world.

Akhirah: everlasting life after death.

Al-Jynayaat: serious crimes where victims can choose to be merciful and receive 'blood money' in compensation.

Al-Mukhalafat: crimes against a state law.

Al Ta'azir: community crimes dealt with by a judge.

Artificial insemination: sperm is medically inserted into the vagina to assist pregnancy.

Artificial insemination by donor (AID): when a woman is made pregnant by the sperm of a man other than her partner, but not through having sexual relations with him.

Artificial insemination by the husband (AIH): when a woman is made pregnant by the sperm of her husband, but not through having sexual relations with him.

Average life expectancy: the average age at which people die.

C

Capital punishment: form of punishment in which a prisoner is put to death for crimes committed. The death penalty.

Cloning: the scientific method by which animals or plants can be created which have exactly the same genetic make-up as the original, because the DNA of the original is used.

Community: a group of people with a common link trying to make things better for each other.

Community service: work which helps the community – sometimes used as a punishment for offenders.

Compassion: a feeling of pity or sympathy that can lead to caring or help.

Conservation: looking after the environment and protecting animals.

Contraception: the artificial and chemical methods used to prevent pregnancy taking place.

Corporal punishment: form of punishment in which pain is inflicted upon a prisoner in order to punish that person for crimes committed.

Crime: the breaking of a state law.

D

Designer babies: babies whose characteristics may be selected by parents to avoid inherited weaknesses or to choose desired physical features.

Deterrence: to put people off committing crimes. One of the aims of punishment.

Disarmament: when a country gets rid of its weapons.

Duty: the moral or legal obligation to do something.

E

Earth Summit: a world conference about the environment.

Embryo: fertilised ovum (egg) at about 12–14 days after conception when implanted into the wall of the womb.

Emergency aid: giving needy people short-term aid as a response to a crisis or disaster, e.g. food in times of famine or war.

Ensoulment: 120 days (or 40 days) after conception, Muslims believe the foetus is given life.

Environmental conservation: looking after the natural resources of the planet by taking steps to conserve them.

Equality: that people should be given the same rights and opportunities regardless of sex, religion, race, etc.

Ethics: the theory relating to what is right and what is wrong behaviour.

Ethnic cleansing: killing or expelling a certain group or race from a country or region.

Euthanasia: inducing a painless death, by agreement and with compassion, to ease suffering. From the Greek meaning 'Good Death'; sometimes called 'Mercy-killing'.

F

Extinction: when all members of a species have died out and that species will never exist on earth again.

Fertility: the ability to produce children.

Fine: money paid as punishment for a crime or other offence.

Forgiveness: to pardon a person for something that they have done wrong.

G

Gambling: playing games of chance to win money.

H

Hadith: the oral tradition relating to the words and deeds of Muhammad.

Hadud: unforgivable crimes with fixed punishments.

Halal: what is allowed in Islam.

Haram: what is forbidden in Islam.

Heterosexual relationship: a sexual relationship with someone of the opposite sex.

Hijab: modest dress for women – often used to mean the veil or headscarf Muslim women wear – means 'cover'.

Homosexual relationship: a sexual relationship with someone of the same sex.

Human genetic engineering: the modification of gene make-up to change the features of a human.

I

Ibadah: worship, all acts of obedience to God.

Illegal drugs: drugs whose possession is against the law.

Infant mortality rate: the rate at which small children die.

In vitro fertilisation (IVF): a scientific method of making a woman pregnant, which does not involve sex. The sperm and egg are fertilised in a Petri dish.

Islam: 1) the name of the religion followed by Muslims; 2) to surrender to the will of Allah (God); 3) peace.

Islamophobia: fear of Islam leading to prejudice against Muslims.

J

Jihad: a struggle against evil. This may be personal or collective.

Judgement: God deciding about individual deeds, good and bad, and rewarding or punishing.

Judgement Day: the day when Allah will judge all people.

Justice: bringing about what is right, fair, according to the law or making up for a wrong that has been committed.

K

Khalifa(h): stewardship. The belief that believers have a duty to look after the environment on behalf of God.

L

Law: rules in a country that govern how people live.

Less Economically Developed Country (LEDC): a country lacking sufficient economic development to lift people out of poverty.

Long-term aid: helping needy people to help themselves by providing the tools, education and funding for projects.

M

Madrassah: a Muslim school attached to a mosque where young Muslims study Islam.

More Economically Developed Country (MEDC): a country where economic development allows people to enjoy a comfortable standard of living.

N

Natural resources: resources like oil, coal, metal ores, gold.

Nuclear proliferation: the increase in the number of countries that have nuclear weapons.

Nuclear war: a war in which the participants use nuclear weapons.

P

Pacifism: the belief that it is unacceptable to take part in war and any other form of violence.

Passive smoking: inhaling smoke from another person's cigarette, cigar or pipe.

Peace: an absence of conflict which leads to happiness and harmony.

Pollution: the act of harming or contaminating the environment.

Prescribed drugs: drugs which are legal, obtained on written instruction of a doctor.

Protection: to stop the criminal hurting anyone in society. An aim of punishment.

Protest: an action to show disagreement with something, for example, government policy.

Punishment: that which is done to a person because they have broken a law.

Q

Quality of life: a measure of fulfilment (how good or bad life is in all its aspects).

Qur'an: the Holy Book revealed to the Prophet Muhammad by the angel Jibril. Allah's final revelation to humankind.

R

Race: a group of people with the same ethnic background.

Reconciliation: when two people or groups of people who have disagreed or fought with each other make up.

Recycling: (the act of) reusing substances to save waste or help the environment.

Reformation: to change someone's behaviour for the better. An aim of punishment.

Reproductive cloning: to make a complete genetically identical animal, possibly a human being.

Resurrection: a belief in life after death.

Retribution: to 'get your own back' on the criminal, based on the teaching of 'an eye for an eye'. An aim of punishment.

S

Sadaqah: voluntary alms giving in addition to zakah.

Sanctity of life: the holiness or sacredness of life.

Saviour siblings: babies conceived so as to provide genetically compatible material for seriously ill relatives.

Self determination: a person's right to choose what happens to them.

Sexual intercourse: the sexual act between two people.

Shari'ah: Islamic law based on the *Qur'an* and Sunnah.

Somatic cell therapy: the repair or replacement of a defective gene within the body.

Stem cell: a cell, most often taken from a 4–5 day old embryo (blastocyst), whose role in the body is yet to be determined.

Stewardship: khalifa(h). The belief that believers have a duty to look after the environment on behalf of God.

Suicide: when a person kills him/herself.

Sunnah: the words and deeds of one Prophet from the *Hadith*.

Surah: a division (chapter) of the *Qur'an*.

Surrogacy: a procedure in which a woman agrees to carry a child conceived artificially for another woman who is unable to do so herself.

Surrogate mother: a woman who has a baby for another woman.

Sustainability: the need to conserve and protect natural resources for future generations.

T

Taqwa: awareness of God.

Tawhid: the oneness of God.

Terrorism: when groups use violence, or the threat of violence, to achieve their aims, rather than using a democratic process. The violence is often indiscriminate and intended to create an atmosphere of fear.

Therapeutic cloning: removing cells from a patient and treating them in a laboratory in order to produce stem cells which may be used to treat disorders, e.g. Alzheimer's disease.

U

Ummah: all Muslims are regarded as part of a brotherhood; the nation of Islam.

Usury: the act of loaning money with excessive interest.

W

World poverty: the idea that the majority of the world's population actually live in conditions of extreme need or hardship.

Z

Zakah: alms giving (charity) of 2.5 per cent of wealth per year.

Index